EDUCATED BUT BROKE

Eliminate your student loans, escape the debt trap and create wealth

John Cook
www.educatedbutbroke.com

REAL REVIEWS

❖ ❖ ❖

Actual feedback for John Cook and *Educated but Broke:*

"As an almost 70 year old man, I think I have some world experience, especially in the field of personal finance. The common myth of making minimum payments on your student loans because it is one of the least expensive loans you'll ever have, has caused an entire generation millions of dollars in lost income potential. Educated and broke does a superb job explaining the mechanics of student loan debt and its true impact. A must read for anyone with debt."- H. Anderson

"Assets are visible, debt is invisible. Educated but broke finally brings light to the darkness of debt" -

Dara M.

"Great book for young people struggling with debt. I wish there was something like this when I was in college" - Jamil A.

"I made many stupid financial decisions when I was younger, and this book is a good summary of all of them. Damn." - Kendall F.

"Apart from all of the quantifiable factors in this book, there is a significant risk carrying around a huge pile of non-dischargeable debt for a decade, particularly when you are young and have zero assets. Not to mention that student loan debt limits your options by forcing you to take the highest paying job regardless of quality of life. Educated but broke is right, pay off those student loans as quickly as you can folks. You will not regret it."
- Greg P.

"I thought I had a basic understanding of my student loan debt, but I have never been able to decipher the details. Educated but Broke is like a magic cipher, made to banish our long standing enemy, the student loan."
- Jennifer F.

"Great read on how financially impossible student loans can be with how interest accrues. I feel like most people have no idea how the mechanics or actual numbers work. I hope this creates a groundswell coming where folks really consider future implications of taking on student loan debt." - Brad B.

"Amazing. Why do we have to be broke to become educated?" - Tamir S.

"Don't get me wrong, even though I was a banker. I despise debt. I do believe that debt, both personal and national debt, will be the demise of this great country. I hope the content in this book can act as a small catalyst to stop the incoming tsunami". - Steven R.

"Thank you for showing people that it is possible to overcome student loan debt." - Seth G.

"Just one chapter of this book could change your life. Don't even waste a second debating it. Just get started.' Goride B.

"It doesn't matter how much money you do or don't make. It doesn't matter how much you have or haven't saved. It doesn't matter how much you are or aren't in debt. Just buy the effing book already!" - A. Sparks

"Educated and broke will provide you an easy to follow guide on how to create a budget where you live on less than you make while also dispelling many of the myths around car loans, credit cards, and student loan interest. For anyone in debt and unsure where to begin, begin with this book" - Brian F.

"This is a new way to look at facing down debt and helping you to live within a budget. It is plain english and contains real examples from John on how he overcame his debt. I recommend this book to anyone struggling with their finances." - Marry M.

"John you are inspiring and Educated but broke is amazing' - Travis B.

Dedicated to the 44 million Americans in $1.7 trillion dollars of student loan debt.

There is a way out.

CONTENTS

Educated but broke

Real reviews

Dedication

This is $170,000 of student loan debt	1
Student loan interest is keeping you broke	7
Opportunity cost and the student interest deductions	15
Your $5.2 million dollar car loan	20
FICO: The greatest scam in modern america	28
Do the unthinkable and Close your credit cards	37
Should you Pay off student loans before you contribute to your 401k?	46
Pay as little as possible by refinancing your student loans	60
The government will not forgive your debt	68
Control your money with a budget	73
A budget in action	78

Your debt free plan vs reality	87
References	99
About the Author	105

THIS IS $170,000 OF STUDENT LOAN DEBT

The only person who sticks closer to you in adversity than a friend is a creditor. - Unknown

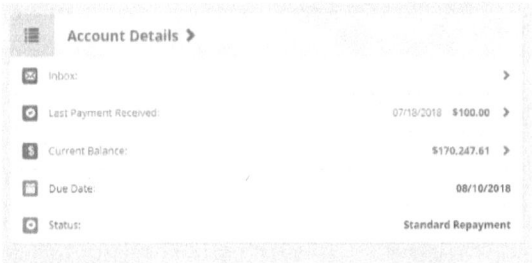

This is what $170,000 of student loan debt looks like. My name is John and in 2018 I owed the US Department of Education and Navient Financial over $170,000 in non-dischargable student loan debt. Non-dischargeable means that unless I die or become physically incapitated, I must pay it back. Since I don't have a death wish, i'm stuck with one option: figure a way out of this nightmare.

I'm one of the 44 million Americans that in aggregate owe $1.7 trillion dollars of student loan debt. I graduated in 2018 with an MBA from a top 20 university and in 2008 with a BS in Computer Science. At the risk of being flamed or turned into a meme on the internet i've decided to write about my student loan debt pay-off journey and what it's like to be educated and broke.

All of my friends have student loan debt. All of them. It's shocking and initiallyhopeless. Student loan debt has become the norm for many 20 to 40 somethings and the idea of living a life without the burden of Sallie Mae or the US Department of Education is laughable. Even talking about paying off your student loan debt early triggers countless eyerolls and the all to common statements like "yeah but we live in _____ (insert any metro city here)" or "we don't make enough money" or "we're waiting for the government to forgive our debt". For a long time, I was part of this group: educated, motivated, dual-income-no-kid couples achieving economic success, who drove nice (leased) cars, while living in rented apartments or lofts that consumed 40% of their post-tax income. Spending alot but saving very little.

My friends and colleagues jokingly called this slice of society the educated and broke. It wasn't well into my early 30s and $170,000 dollars of student loan debt later, did I realize that I was one of them. I've decided to share my story to encourage an open discussion on not only the quantity of debt college graduates have, but how to solve it.

The topic of student loans has been a social pariah, a faux pas, something we avoid talking about. This makes no sense, there is a 1 in 7 chance that the person you're talking with has student loan debt. When we expand this figure to include all types of debt, there is an 80% chance that your neighbor, colleague, boss or friend is suffering from the same financial hardship as you. My financial hardship, according to the US Department of Education is as follows:

Student Loan Hell

Original Principal Balance:	$ 169,724.40
Standard Monthly Payment:	$ 2,002.00
Number of Months:	120
Total Amount Paid:	$ 240,240.00
Interest Paid	$ 70,515.60

Unfortunately my story is not uncommon, the financial profile of a typical American is bleak, consider these 10 facts of American consumer debt:

1. Americans have $12.58 trillion dollars in

consumer debt.

2. It will take 18 years to pay off the average credit card balance.

3. 1 out of 4 Americans have more in debt than savings.

4. Americans have $1.7 trillion dollars of student loan debt.

5. 73% of Americans die with debt.

6. Americans have over $1.6 trillion dollars of auto loans with an average payment of $508 a month.

7. On average, each household with a credit card carries $8,284 in credit card debt.

8. 72% of Americans feel "stressed out" about debt and 22% feel "extreme" stress over the finances.

9. 1 out of 10 people with student loan debt will default on a payment at some point in their life.

10. Only one percent of individuals eligible for the "Federal Loan Forgiveness Program" actually had their student loans forgiven

I will show you that whether you have $5,000, $50,000 or $150,000 (or higher) of student loan debt, it is possible to pay it off without joining the Public Service Loan Forgiveness (bulletpoint #10) program extending payments to 30 years via IBR. But to achieve this, it will require sacrifice, a detailed budget, and alot of cash. If you follow the framework outlined in this book, you will pay off your debt, and you will become debt free. Here's the proof:

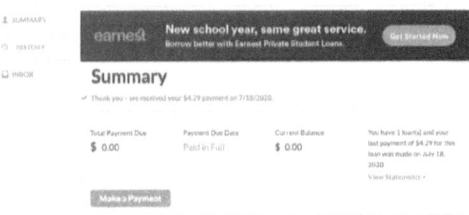

This is an actual screenshot of the amount of student loan debt I still owe. In less than 24 months I went from drowning in $170,000 of debt to being 100% debt free. To help you achieve a similar goal, we'll cover 8 concepts that will take you from powerless to empowered:

1. Why your student loan interest is keeping you broke
2. The true cost of missed wealth creation opportunities 3. FICO: the greatest scam in modern America
4. Credit cards are the cigarettes of wealth creation
5. Ending the "contribute to your retirement first" myth
6. Refinancing debt to minimize lost opportunity cost
7. Accept that the government will never forgive your debt, and what to do now
8. Turn your money into more money with a budget

There is a clear path to financial freedom and you

can do it, but it will require sacrifice. Creating wealth is hard. Being broke is hard. Choose your hard.

John Cook
San Francsico, CA

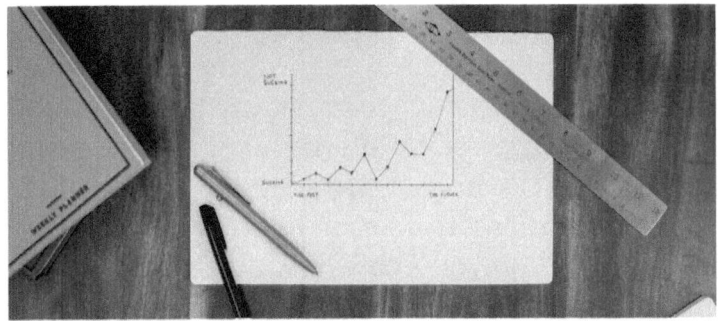

STUDENT LOAN INTEREST IS KEEPING YOU BROKE

*Interest is the eighth wonder of the world.
Those who understands it, earn it ... those
who doesn't ... pay it. - Albert Einstein*

When I look back on the level of effort it took for me to acquire $170,000 of student loan debt, it's quite frankly shocking at how easy it was. A 'pre-entrance loan counseling' online class, a couple of digital signatures, and like digital magic, the transaction was complete. What I continue to struggle with is the understanding that although it is easy to get into student loan debt, the path out is difficult.

One of the key metrics in quantifying the difficulty of conquering student loan debt is to understand the impact interest has on the loan...I mean really understand the impact. Do you know how much interest accrues within each loan daily, weekly, or even yearly? Do you know how much of your payment is applied to interest vs. principal? Fear not, by the end of this chapter you will be able to calculate, to the penny, how much interest you pay per loan per day, week, month and year.

First let's define principal , interest and accrued interest.

Principal refers to the original sum of money borrowed to attend college. In my example, I borrowed $169,724 to get an MBA from USC and a BS in Computer Science. My principal amount owed is $169,724.

Interest refers to the sum of money paid to the lender (US Department of Education, Navigant Financial, Sallie Mae, etc) for the privledge of using (borrwing) their money. Interest is defined as a percentage. The interest of my student loans varied from 5.31% to 7.00%. If I took 10 years to pay off the $169,724 via standard payment plan I would have paid $70,515 in interest.

Accrued interest is the interest on the principal

(the original loan amount) which has been added to the principal. Yes, this is interest on interest and is part of the reason why your loan amount never goes down when you make minimum monthly payments.

You "accrue interest" when your student loan is in any type of non-payment status e.g. "in school", "grace period", "deferment", "forebarance". It is the point in time after your loan has been disbursed but before you begin payment. For most of us, we accrue interest when we are in school.

Interest accrues daily on your loan when a payment is not required (as we just discussed). Accrued interest is **capitalized** (added to the principal balance) when the loan goes into repayment thereby increasing the total outstanding balance due and the amount of interest which accrues daily. Because interest continues to accrue on the principal balance, any future interest that accrues after capitalization event will be based on the new outstanding principal amount (previous principal balance plus capitalized interest). Therefore, capitalization increases the total cost of your loan. Let's work through a real life example using a $20,500 student loan I borrowed in 2017 at an interest rate of 6.00%.

1. I borrowed $20,500 in late 2017. This is the **principal amount.**
2. I didn't begin repayments on this loan until 2019.

3. Between 2017 and 2019 this loan accrued $895.94 of interest, this is "**accrued interest**".

4. When repayment of the student loan was initiated in 2019, the accrued interest ($895.94) was added (capitalized) to the principal amount.

5. The new amount owed is $21,395.94 ($20,500 + $895.94)

6. Interest is charged on the new amount. This is interest on interest. Its why the bank has a big building in your city skyline and you live in an apartment with 2 roommates.

The table below outlines this math.

	With accured interest	Without accrued interest
Original Amount	$ 20,500.00	$ 20,500.00
Accured Interest	$ 895.94	$ -
New Amount	$ 21,395.94	$ 20,500.00
Interest Rate	6.00%	6.00%
Annual interest on new amount (New amount * Interest Rate)	$ 1,283.76	$ 1,230.00

My monthly payment now goes up by $53.76 ($1283.76-$1230.00). What's more important is that interest now accrues on the the new principal amount — in this example $21,395.94.

This is why some people make payments on student loans but the debt never goes down, the amount paid does not offset the accrued interest which is capitalized on the loan. You need to know how to calculate interest to avoid these type of financial death traps.

Let's calculate student loan interest:

In this example we'll use the outstanding balance student loan balance I had at the time of writing: $154,793.48. I want you to follow along your current outstading balance. Here's the breakdown of the individual student loans and the aggregate total.

Department of Education Loan Group	Due Date	Interest Rate	Monthly Payment	Original Loan Amount	Outstanding Principal
B	7/10/18	6.31%	$ 235.08	$ 18,170.06	$ 18,170.06
D	2/10/19	5.31%	$ 245.42	$ 20,500.11	$ 20,500.00
F	7/10/18	6.51%	$ 427.18	$ 34,018.06	$ 34,018.06
G	7/10/18	7.00%	$ 465.32	$ 36,605.07	$ 36,605.07
H	2/10/19	6.00%	$ 244.28	$ 25,500.12	$ 20,500.00
I	7/10/18	7.00%	$ 308.58	$ 25,000.17	$ 25,000.07
		Total:	$ 1,925.86	$ 159,793.59	$ 154,793.26

Step 1: List all of your individual student loans in a spreadsheet like excel.

Recreate the table I just created, but using your individual student loans. Some loan servicing providers like Edfinancial organize individual student loans into 'groups' based on disbursement date. For example, group G above is actually two individual loans related to tuition for a fall semester at USC. Keep it simple, the excel file just needs 2 columns: interest rate, outstanding principal.

Step 2: Calculate the daily interest rate of each loan group.

Do this for each loan. If your speadsheet has six

lines, you will need to calculate this six times. Using my group G as an example, the annual interest rate for that loan group is 7.00% This means the $36,000 loan I received will have a balance of $38,520 365 days after the disbursement date as outlined below. This table outlines how I calculated the $38,520 figure.

Interest calculation on a $36,000 student loan at 7.00%		
Principal amount owed on (1/1/2018)	$	36,000.00
Interest Rate		7.00%
Daily Interest Rate (7.00/365 days)		0.02%
Interest accrued by 1/1/2019 (Principal & Interest)	$	2,520.00
New Balance on 1/1/2019	$	38,520.00

You can see we calculated the daily interest rate by taking the Annual interest rate (7.00%) and dividing by 365 days. The daily interest rate on a 7.00% loan is .02% or 1/5 of one percent. When we apply this to the $154,000 principal balance across my aggregate loan groups you can see my daily interest rate hovers between 0.01 and almost .020 as outlined below.

Department of Education Loan Group	Due Date	Interest Rate	Daily Interest	Monthly Payment	Original Loan Amount	Outstanding Principal
B	7/10/18	6.31%	0.02%	$ 235.08	$ 18,170.06	$ 18,170.06
D	2/10/19	5.31%	0.01%	$ 245.42	$ 20,500.11	$ 20,500.00
F	7/10/18	6.51%	0.02%	$ 427.18	$ 34,018.06	$ 34,018.06
G	7/10/18	7.00%	0.02%	$ 465.32	$ 36,605.07	$ 36,605.07
H	2/10/19	6.00%	0.02%	$ 244.28	$ 25,500.12	$ 20,500.00
I	7/10/18	7.00%	0.02%	$ 308.58	$ 25,000.17	$ 25,000.07
		Total:		$ 1,925.86	$ 159,793.59	$ 154,793.26

This means that for every dollar I give to the US Department of Education almost 2 cents is allocated to interest. This doesn't sound like alot, but with big numbers it's huge! Keep reading.

Step 3. Multiple the daily interest rate by the outstanding balance.

Here's where the numbers get shocking. I can actually see how much interest my student loans accrue everyday by multiplying the daily interest rate by the outstanding balance (Daily Interest Rate * Outstanding Principal).

Department of Education Loan Group	Due Date	Interest Rate	Daily Interest	Daily Interest Amount	Monthly Payment	Original Loan Amount	Outstanding Principal
B	7/10/18	6.31%	0.02%	$ 3.14	$ 235.08	$ 18,170.06	$ 18,170.06
D	2/10/19	5.31%	0.01%	$ 2.98	$ 245.42	$ 20,500.11	$ 20,500.00
F	7/10/18	6.51%	0.02%	$ 6.07	$ 427.18	$ 34,018.06	$ 34,018.06
G	7/10/18	7.00%	0.02%	$ 7.02	$ 465.32	$ 36,605.07	$ 36,605.07
H	2/10/19	6.00%	0.02%	$ 3.37	$ 244.28	$ 25,500.12	$ 20,500.00
I	7/10/18	7.00%	0.02%	$ 4.79	$ 308.58	$ 25,000.17	$ 25,000.07
	Total:			$ 27.38	$ 1,925.86	$ 159,793.59	$ 154,793.26

The $154,793 principal balance accrues over $27 a day in interest alone. This is quite concerning considering my first job out of high school paid $5.75 an hour!

Step 4. Multiply the daily interest amount by 30 days.

This calculation will give you the approximate interest each loan group accrues in a 30 day window. My $154,000 of student loan debt will accrue approximately $815 of interest in 30 days.

Department of Education Loan Group	Due Date	Interest Rate	Daily Interest	Daily Interest Amount	30 Day Interest Amount	Monthly Payment	Original Loan Amount	Outstanding Principal
B	7/10/18	6.31%	0.02%	$ 3.14	$ 94.24	$ 235.08	$ 18,170.06	$ 18,170.06
D	2/10/19	5.31%	0.01%	$ 2.98	$ 89.47	$ 245.42	$ 20,500.11	$ 20,500.00
F	7/10/18	6.51%	0.02%	$ 6.07	$ 182.02	$ 427.18	$ 34,018.06	$ 34,018.06
G	7/10/18	7.00%	0.02%	$ 7.01	$ 210.60	$ 465.32	$ 36,605.07	$ 36,605.07
H	2/10/19	6.00%	0.02%	$ 3.37	$ 101.10	$ 244.28	$ 25,500.12	$ 20,500.00
I	7/10/18	7.00%	0.02%	$ 4.79	$ 143.84	$ 308.58	$ 25,000.17	$ 25,000.07
	Total:			$ 27.38	$ 821.26	$ 1,925.86	$ 159,793.59	$ 154,793.26

When we wonder why our student loan balance

never go down, especially in the beginning, this is it! Initial repayment plans have over 50% of the payment balance going towards interest. The only path to reducing the interest payment is by making additional payments to principal.

Conclusion: If you do not understand how interest is calculated on your student loans, you will never get out of debt.

The $27 daily interest and $815/monthly interest is mind numbing. Calculate the daily and monthly interest on your loans. If you are one of the 44 million Americans For the 44 million Americans who have over $1.5 trillion dollars of student loan debt, this is your wake up call. Be intentional, be focused, live on less than what you earn and stop paying interest on interest.

OPPORTUNITY COST AND THE STUDENT INTEREST DEDUCTIONS

Nothing is more expensive than a missed opportunity. - H Jackson Brown

Deducting student loan interest on your tax return is a joke. It is a scam designed to keep the poor from climbing out of poverty and the middle class stuck in the middle. More and more I hear comments like "Don't pay off your student loans, just make the minimum payments and deduct the interest!" This is right towards the top of the stupid scale and this myth needs to be debunked. Deducting your student loan interest is not saving you money. There are 2 only things you can do to save money on student loans:

1. Avoid student loans at all costs.
2. Pay off your student loans as quickly as possible.

I am going to assume that you are one of the 44 million Americans who has student loan debt, therefore you belong in the bucket "Pay off your student loans as quickly as possible". There is no other option, it is literally that simple and here is why:

You always pay more interest than you save.

The bottom line is that opting to deduct your student loan interest instead of paying it off as quickly as possible is a bad idea because you always pay more in interest than you save. I won't get into the minutia about itemizing your taxes, adjusted gross income, head of household or anything else because quite frankly it doesn't matter.

There is no scenario in which it is more advantageous to deduct loan interest on your tax return instead of paying it off. Let's prove this by looking at the student loan debt profile of a typical American: an individual with $50,000 of student loan debt who makes a pre-tax (gross) income of $80,000 / annually, outlined below.

Typical American with student loan debt	
Student Loan Amount:	$50,000
Interest Rate:	5.00%
Annual Interest Paid:	$2,500
Gross (Pre-tax) Income:	$80,000

IRS guidelines dictate that you can deduct up to $2,500 of your student loan interest if you're single. When you 'deduct' something from your gross income, it just means your gross income goes down. This is good because it means you pay fewer taxes to the US Government and since the US Government couldn't balance a household budget, you certainly don't want them handling your money. You can see the impact in the table below, the gross income of this individual dropped from $80,000 to $77,500.

Impact of deduction to pre-tax income	
Pre-tax income before deduction:	$80,000
Amount deducted from pre-tax income:	$2,500
Pre-tax income after deduction:	$77,500

The 2020 federal tax bracket for individuals who make between $39,475 and $84,200 is 24%. This means that the federal government seizes 24 cents of every dollar you earn. Reducing the gross income from $80,000 to $77,500 means that no tax is being paid on $2,500 of the income you earned because it was "deducted away". The net impact is that you avoid paying $600 of federal income tax as outlined below ($2,500*.24). Although i'm happy to see that we were able to avoid paying the Internal Revenue Service $600, we've actually paid the US Department of Education $2,500 in interest!

Impact of deduction to pre-tax income	
Amount deducted from gross income:	$2,500
Federal income tax rate	24.00%
Pre-tax income after deduction:	$600

Let that sink in, we paid $2,500 of interest to avoid paying $600 of taxes.

This is the dilemma of the educated and broke. We think we're winning by deducting interest, mak-

Deducting student loan interest is still a bad idea	
Amount paid in interest	$2,500
Amount avoided in taxes	$600
Net loss	($1,900)

ing minimum student loan payments and investing the difference in the stock market. We think that these activities will somehow yield a more optimistic outcome, a path to financial independence, but that logic is wrong.

It's the same logic followed by the majority of Americans, yet 8 out of 10 of us can't afford our next major emergency, 1 out of 4 of us have more in debt than in retirement and our average car payment is over $500 a month! This is the insanity of the new normal and normal is broke. Normal sucks.

Conclusion: You do not have save money by deducting your student loan interest.

If you're still on the fence about student loan debt, if you're still asking yourself "Should I pay off my student loan debt early", the answer is clear: pay off your student loan debt as quickly as possible. It is the only path to financial independence. If you want to be broke (normal), please deduct your student loan interest on your tax return. If you're tired of being educated but broke, make a resolution to pay off your student loan debt as quickly as possible.

YOUR $5.2 MILLION DOLLAR CAR LOAN

Wonder why you're broke? Look in the driveway.
- Dave Ramsey

I am about to share a scary story. A real story, that happened to me, and is probably happening to you. A mind-numbing 107 million Americans owe in aggregate $568 billion in auto debt. The aggregate amount borrowed has increased year/over/year, 7 years in a row.

Americans with Auto Debt

# Americans with a car loan	$ 107,000,000.00
Total outstanding car loan debt balance	$ 568,000,000,000.00
Average debt per car owner	$ 5,308.41

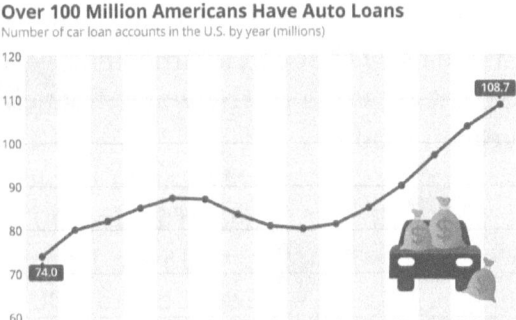

The purpose of this post is not to diminish or harp on the 1/3rd of us who have auto debt. We all already know its a terrible idea. I'm going to show you why auto debt is a limiting factor to wealth creation, a mechanism to keep the middle class in the middle, and the upper middle class from climbing the economic ladder.

More specifically, I'm going to show you why my 2003 Nissan 350z which I financed for $16,000 really cost me $5.2 million, and why your car loan probably cost you the same, if not more.

Meet my baby — Lindsay Lohan

In 2007, I was offered a job at the age of 21 making $22/ hour full time. I thought I was amazing, positioned to climb the career ladder. My first order of business, go buy a car to show people that I didn't know just-how-awesome-I-am. I drove my beater at the time, a 1989 Mitsubishi Galant to a local Sacramento dealership and swore to myself it would be the last time I saw that car. In hindsight, getting rid of the Galant was one of the worst financial decisions i've ever made.

My car of choice at the age of 21 in 2007? A Nissan 350z. Not just any 350z, but a 2004 Nissan 350z enthusiast edition. Complete with custom leather trip, an upgraded Bose sound system and custom rims.

Wealthy people ask "How much?" but Poor people ask "How much per month?"

I think a big mistake I made was asking the wrong question. I didn't ask 'If I could afford the car', instead I asked — can I afford the car payment? This stupid question is what sets most Americans, including me, into what we call the perpetual ratrace: buying things we can't afford to impress people we don't like which forces us to stay at a job we hate.

A couple test drives and a quick discussion with the finance manager, I was approved for an $18,000 48 month car loan with a $2,000 down payment + trade in. The economics of this deal sucked, and looking back, it was a complete rip-off. $15,000 cash in hand would have taken the car off the lot, but instead, I was ripped on two fronts:

1. On the front end: The total purchase payment of the car was higher than the book value.
2. On the back end: The aggregate interest required to pay off the overpriced car payment.

Most consumers think this is where the pain ends. Oh no, car loans, MY car loan, cost in aggregate $5.2 million dollars in lost opportunity.

Where did the $5.2 million go?

Let's run some numbers to prove out the $5.2 million dollars in lost opportunity. As a recap, my monthly payment was $368. At the age of 21, full coverage insurance for a sports car ran ~ $240 / month. In aggregate, the $608 represents approximately $7,296 a year.

Your car is the reason you're broke

Monthly Car Note	$ 368.00
Monthly Insurance	$ 240.00
Total Monthly Payment	$ 608.00

What if, instead of financing a car, I took the $608 / month or $7,296 / year and invested it for 4 years (the duration of the car loan)....and then NEVER invested another penny. Let me recap that, for 48 months I save $608, and starting at month 49 I never save or invest another PENNY. By the age of 65, How much would I have? $500,000? 1 million? Try again. How about $5.2 million.

How is this possible? The answer is compound interest. Compound interest is where your money makes money. Don't believe me? You can calculate it yourself:

How a $600 car payment turns into $5 million dollars

Age	Additional Amount Invested	Total Amount
19	$7,296	$ 8,171.52
20	$7,296	$ 17,323.62
21	$7,296	$ 27,573.98
22	$7,296	$ 39,054.37
23	$0	$ 43,740.90
24	$0	$ 48,989.81
25	$0	$ 54,868.58
30	$0	$ 96,697.19
40	$0	$ 300,326.80
50	$0	$ 932,769.46
60	$0	$ 2,897,040.36
61	$0	$ 3,244,685.21
62	$0	$ 3,634,047.43
63	$0	$ 4,070,133.12
64	$0	$ 4,558,549.10
65	$0	$ 5,105,574.99

Year 1: Take the "Additional Amount Invested"($7,296) and multiply it by 1.12. In this example, I assume a 12% rate of return.

Year 2:Take the year 1 year 'Total Amount", add it to the year 2 "Additional Amount invested" and multiply that result by 1.12.

Year 3: and beyond: Take the year 2 'Total Amount", add it to the year 3 "Additional Amount invested" and multiply that result by 1.12.

You can see what's happening here: the interest from year 1 is being added to the principal amount invested at the end of year 1. Compound interest is then applied to that result, which produced in aggregate 5.2 million dollars over this 44-year window!

Is a 12% rate of return realistic?

I challenge and disagree with the statement that a 12% return over an aggregate period is unrealistic. The S&P500 (an index of the 500 largest U.S. publicly traded companies) has produced ~ 11% return on investment over the past 18 years..and using a quick fund scan, here is a simple portfolio of 4 mutual funds (Portfolio 1) which have exceeded the S&P500 Index (Portfolio 2) and produced an arithmetic average > 12% (back-tested from 1/06 to 12/18):

Ticker	Name	Allocation
FKSCX	Franklin Intl Small Cap Adv	25.00%
BCSIX	Brown Capital Mgmt Small Co Inv	25.00%
JVAIX	JPMorgan Value Advantage L	25.00%
PARWX	Parnassus Endeavor Investor	25.00%

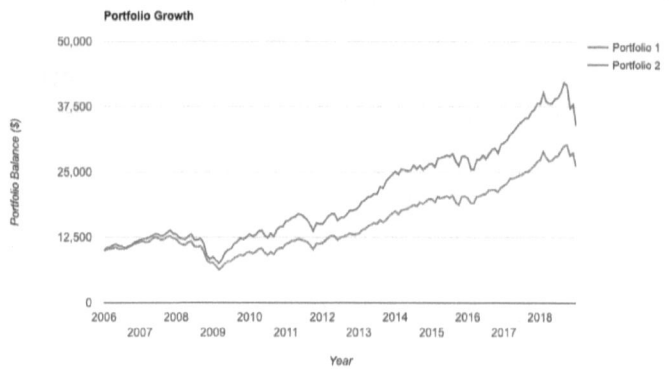

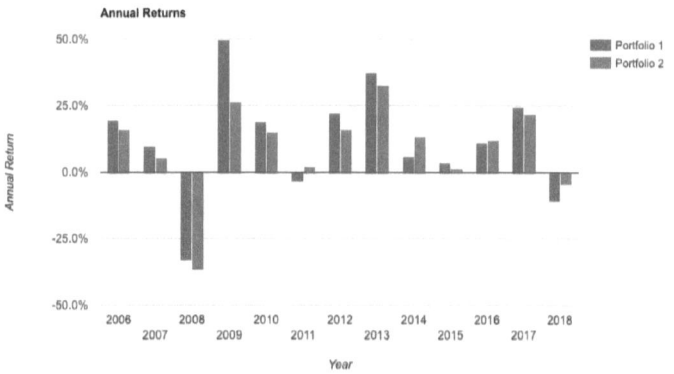

But alas, let's say that 12% is not possible in today's economic climate…so what. If i'm only half right, you'll still have $2.5 million in your savings account by the age of 65! Don't believe me? Goto www.portfoliovisualizer.com and see for yourself!

Conclusion: Avoid car loans, pay with cash.

Was my car worth it? Was my baby, Lindsay Lohan,

my Nissan 350z enthusiast edition worth it? Not by a long shot. If I could undo the hands of time, I would have re-allocated $2,000 or so on the Galant and pocketed the rest. That's unfortunately not the card I dealt myself, but going forward, I will never make this mistake again, and it's a mistake you should avoid as well.

Want to avoid the educated and broke trap? Avoid car loans, pay with cash. Car loans are a tool designed to keep poor people poor and the middle class from climbing the socioeconomic ladder.

Car loans are the number one reason why the typical American has no money in retirement. If you invested your six year car payment into your retirement account, then never saved another penny for the rest of your life, you would have over $5.2 million dollars. Hope you like car.

FICO: THE GREATEST SCAM IN MODERN AMERICA

When I was young, people lived from paycheck to paycheck. Today, it seems like they live from credit card payment to credit card payment. - Robert Kiyosaki

Before I spend the next chapter slamming credit scores, FICO (Short for Fair Isaac Corporation, the largest and best known private company that privdes software for calculating a person's credit score) and the financial services credit card industry in general, I will admit that I was once amendment about having a high credit score:

1. I thought a high credit score was a meaningful in-

dicator of financial success.
2. I thought a high credit score was an indicator of upward mobility.
3. I thought a high credit score was the pre-requisite to wealth.

When I turned 18, I opened my first credit card with 1st Financial Bank, who gave me a whopping $150 credit line. Like a good consumer, I grew that line of credit and a few others to around a little over $100,000 of available credit over a 10 year period as shown below:

Bank of America	$ 27,000.00
First Financial	$ 17,400.00
Chase	$ 11,000.00
American Express	$ 32,795.00
Sacramento Credit Union	$ 14,000.00
Total available credit:	$ 102,195.00

Then I looked up at the age of 30 and asked myself:

"Where the hell is all my money going?"

This awesome line of consumer credit did not make me rich, produce any passive income, or act as a "catalyst" to wealth creation. Credit cards do the opposite. Credit cards keep the middle class, in the middle class and prevent the working poor from entering the middle class. The most effective tool you and I have to create wealth is our income. Yet how are we supposed to 'build wealth' when the average American owes $5,700 and Californians owing $10,496?

When your money is tied up in credit card and student loan payments, you can't create wealth. I recently thought about how this applied to my personal life and came to the following conclusion: Credit cards serve no purpose in my life. I can live without credit cards. The idea that I need to 'build credit' to have a good life is a joke and fake reality brought to us by FICO.

Case in point: My 801 credit score. I had $170,000 of student loan debt and an 801 credit score. Let me repeat that: $170,000 of student loan debt = 801 credit score.

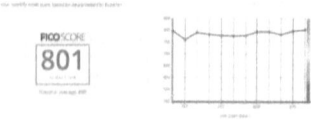

Your credit score is not a measurement of wealth. Your credit score is not a measurement of your success. Your credit score is not a measurement of how much money you make.

Your credit score is a measurement of your ability to pay debt.

Why do we want to build credit? So we can borrow debt. Why do we want to borrow debt? So we can build credit. Why do want to build credit? So we can borrow debt. This, ladies and gentlemen of the internet, is the credit score hamster wheel.

The blogs telling you to "build a good credit score", all have credit card advertisements. They are not looking out in your best interest. You do not need to build a good credit score. You do not need any credit score. You can live a life within your means, without a credit card. Your personal visa debit card offers the same protection as a credit card. You do not need a high credit score to achieve home ownership and obtain a mortgage. It is quite common for mortgage lenders to engage in a process called manual underwriting. Manual underwriting is a manual process of evaluating your ability to repay a loan. Instead of the decision being left to a computer algorithm (FICO score), an individual or group of individuals review your finances in detail to determine whether or not your application should be approved.

But what about credit card reward points?

I average over $100,000 annually on an American Express card that converts points to gift cards and I get about $1,000 a year cash back. That's one percent folks. $1,000 sounds great right? Well considering that consumers spend 10%-17% more on average w/ credit cards than with cash, it's really a terrible idea. Think about it another way, American Express is paying me $1,000 at the end of the year for over-paying anywhere from $10,000 to $17,000. Would you give me $17,000 today if I promised to give you back $1,000 in 12 months?

Absolutely not. I know these are touchy statements, and I know there's a bunch of know-it-alls who will scream at the top of their lungs:

"NOT ME JOHN...NOT ME, I USE CREDIT CARDS FOR POINTS. I PAY MY BALANCE IN FULL EVERY MONTH!"

The unfortunate reality is that point redemption on most cards is ONE PERCENT OF ONE DOLLAR. Do you know what that means? You need to spend one hundred thousand dollars to earn one thousand dollars.

"BUT JOHN ..I GET 2%..3.%..5% CASH BACK ON MY CARDS!! I'M WINNING!"

Review this table to really understand how much money you're "making" from your credit card cash back program. Not a whole lot. It's not worth the gyrations of reconciling against your bank account. Have you ever met a millionaire who said: "The reason I became rich is be-

Amount Spent:	$1,000.00	$10,000.00	$25,000.00	$100,000.00
1% Cash Back	$10.00	$100.00	$250.00	$1,000.00
2% Cash Back	$20.00	$500.00	$500.00	$2,000.00
5% Cash Back	$50.00	$1,250.00	$1,250.00	$5,000.00

cause of my visa points"? I haven't. Not one. You spend more money when you use your credit cards. This is a fact. One of the most often cited studies is one conducted by Dun & Bradstreet, where the company found that people spend 12–18% more when using credit cards instead of cash. McDonald's reports its average ticket is $7 when people use credit cards versus $4.50 for cash. So we spend 12% to 18% more to earn 5% cash back? No thanks. You're not winning, i'm not winning, no one is winning with credit cards. The only people who are winning are Visa, Mastercard and American Express.

1. Americans have in aggregate $830 billion of credit card debt, that's $8,161 per household
2. 20% of Americans have more in credit card debt than in retirement

Do you think it's possible to live a life without credit cards, but you're scared to take the leap? Keep reading.

Balance transfers don't do anything. You're still broke.

How do I know? Because I was the king of balance transfers. The culmination of happiness when I made my last and final payment to Chase Credit cards is depicted below.

My balance transfer journey began in August 2017 when I thought it would be a fantastic idea to initiate a $10,267 credit card balance transfer from Bank of America to Chase. The illusion of debt consolidation or balance transfers as a means to manage debt is just that -an illusion.

YOUR ACCOUNT MESSAGES		

You have one or more balance(s) with APR expiration dates, as shown in the Interest Charge section. These APRs will continue through the expiration dates shown in the Interest Charges section.

ACCOUNT ACTIVITY		
Date of Transaction	Merchant Name or Transaction Description	$ Amount
BALANCE TRANSFERS		
06/18	BALANCE TRANSFER TO ▬▬▬	3,707.00
06/18	BALANCE TRANSFER TO ▬▬▬	8,560.00

Immediately after the balance transfer, I sighed with relief thinking that I made meaningful progress in my debt freedom journey. When the reality is that 0 net progress had been made. So what did I do? Make minimum payments for almost 12 months! In fact I didn't step it into high gear until the last 5 months. Literally 98% of the debt was paid off in Spring/Summer 2018.

Payment date	Status		Amount
Aug 24, 2018	Completed	▸ See details	$1,419.71
Aug 5, 2018	Completed	▸ See details	$4,000.00
Jul 22, 2018	Completed	▸ See details	$1,668.29
Jun 21, 2018	Completed	▸ See details	$1,200.00
Jun 2, 2018	Completed	▸ See details	$550.00
Jun 1, 2018	Completed	▸ See details	$1,000.00
May 3, 2018	Completed	▸ See details	$99.00
Apr 3, 2018	Completed	▸ See details	$100.00
Mar 2, 2018	Completed	▸ See details	$101.00
Feb 2, 2018	Completed	▸ See details	$102.00
Jan 3, 2018	Completed	▸ See details	$103.00
Dec 3, 2017	Completed	▸ See details	$104.00
Nov 3, 2017	Completed	▸ See details	$105.00
Oct 3, 2017	Completed	▸ See details	$106.00
Sep 3, 2017	Completed	▸ See details	$107.00
Aug 3, 2017	Completed	▸ See details	$102.00

Balance transfers will not make a meaningful impact in your debt payoff journey. It certainly didn't in mine. What made the most impact was the desire and focus to get out of credit card debt. If I were going to keep the debt for 30 years, then yes, the balance transfer and interest rates matter. Interest rates become a huge problem. The big problem with balance transfers is I felt like I actually did something. This made me take my eye off the ball and enabled me to be less than laser focused. That's 98% of getting out of debt. Two percent of getting out of debt is interest rate.

My steps to paying off this debt were super simple and largely unscientific. I didn't spend too much time weighing the pro/cons because my goal was to pay off in < 12 months.

1. I lived on 50% of my take home income of the 4 months leading up to the 0 balance.
2. I created a written budget, and followed it to the penny.
3. I had plastic surgery and cut up my credit cards, swearing never to use it again.

Conclusion: Make FICO think you're dead.

If you want to go on vacation, pay with cash. If you're worried about a $500 rental car hold on your checking account, then seriously, you can't afford the vacation. Credit cards are the cigarettes of the financial services industry. It will kill you. It is killing all of us. 80% of Americans carry debt, and 20% of Americans have more credit card debt than savings Build a life with no credit. Don't accept the idea of "building good credit". There is no such thing as good credit, because credit = debt. Use your income to create wealth, not pay debt. If you don't, you'll end up with an 800 credit score and $170,000 in debt.

DO THE UNTHINKABLE AND CLOSE YOUR CREDIT CARDS

Paint or get off the ladder. - Unknown

I know closing your credit cards sounds scary. Your sisters, brothers, friends, families and crazy Uncle Tom have all engrained a mindset of "credit worthiness" into your spirit. I promise you it's not scary, and once you're on the other side your only regret will be you wishing you didn't take the leap sooner. Want proof? I am going to show what happens to your credit score when you decide to close all of your credit cards and choose a life of freedom, a life without debt.

This is not a theoretical activity or a 'what-if', this is something I consciously chose to do. In July 2018 I had approximately $102,000 of available credit. As of December 2018, all of these accounts are closed.

Bank of America	$ 27,000.00
First Financial	$ 17,400.00
Chase	$ 11,000.00
American Express	$ 32,795.00
Sacramento Credit Union	$ 14,000.00
Total available credit:	$ 102,195.00

I closed all 5 of my credit cards to see what happens to my 800 credit score. Am I crazy? Maybe, but with 8/10 Americans living pay check to pay check and unable to afford the next $500 emergency, I've come to realization that what we're doing, what the typical american is doing, what I've been doing, just isn't working. So let me be crystal clear:

    1. Credit cards are the cigarettes of the financial services industry.
    2. Credit cards keep poor people poor.
    3. Credit cards keep the middle class from climbing the economic ladder.

FICO system are not a measurement of wealth, financial success, or economic independence. Credit cards and the FICO system measure your ability to borrow debt, and pay it back. Why do we want a high FICO score? So we can borrow money. Why do we want to borrow money? So we can have a high FICO score. Why do we want a high FICO score? So we can borrow money. This my friends, is the rat race of credit card debt, and my 800 credit score is the carrot:

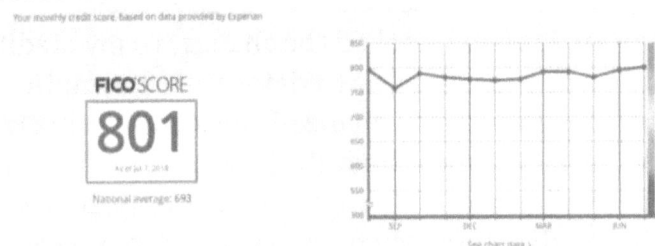

What happen to my FICO score when I closed my credit cards?

Let me preface this by saying, closing your credit cards is hard. I had to call each bank 1 by 1, and explain to no fewer than 3 people per bank that I was adamant about closing my account. Each call required multiple escalations. American Express even said (not making this up):

> *"I am making a huge mistake by closing my $33,000 line of credit".*

My local credit union, wouldn't even let me close the account over the phone. I had to drive to their HQ, get a certified letter, and speak to the branch manager. Who said (i'm quoting this!):

"John you've had this credit card for 13 years, you're making a big mistake by closing this account".

I laughed and said, "the only path to financial freedom is one without credit". He promptly closed the account and we wished each other good luck.

Out of curiosity I tracked the changes to my credit score on a monthly basis to determine its implications. The first major change I noticed was in December 2019, approximately 6 months later, with $0 in available credit, living a cash only budget, with a small emergency fund — my FICO score went from 800 to 764.

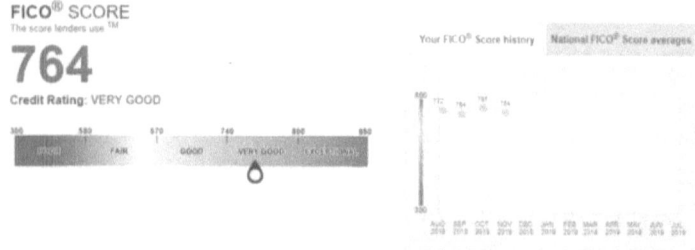

To understand *why* my score went down 36 points, I pulled a credit report from www.annualcreditreport.com (this is the only free credit report web site on the internet, authorized by the federal government. Everything else is private, costs $$ and is for-profit). Here's what I found:

Account Type	Open	With Balance	Total Balance	Available	Credit Limit	Debt to Credit	Payment
Revolving	2	0	$0	$31,100	$31,100	0.0%	$0
Mortgage							
Installment	10	10	$166,972	-$6,929	$160,043	104.0%	$0
Other							
Total	12	10	$166,972	$24,171	$191,143	87.0%	$0

With my student loans accruing interest at an approximate rate of $27/day, the interest capitalized to the principal produced a total balance *higher* than the original loan amount. The net of this is a debt-to-credit ratio > 100%. With a high debt-to-credit ratio, your FICO score drops — mine certainly did. Quite frankly, I don't care that my debt-to-credit ratio is > 100% because my end goal is to be 100% debt free with an 'indeterminable' credit score. This should be your goal as well.

After the low of 747 in December 2019, I noticed an uptick in credit score depsite closing all of my consumer accounts. As of June 2020 the score stands at 830:

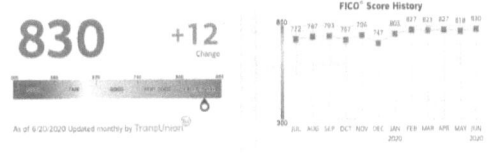

Interesting observation right? My available line of credit (previous $102,195) was reduced to $0 as a result of me closing all my accounts. Yet after the initial dip to 747, my credit score increases to a record high of 830. Do not fall into the trap of chasing a high credit score by keeping credit cards open, paying it off everything, or any other similar gyrations we've heard a million times. It is a scam designed to keep you poor. This is the proof.

You do not need to have one, five or ten credit cards open at any given time. In fact you shouldn't. Your credit score is not a measurement of your wealth. It has never been, and it will never be. Your measurement of wealth is defined by the amount of cash and incoming producing assets you have in your possession. But don't fret, closing your credit cards does not religate you to a pitiful life void of joy hand happiness, quite the opposite.

How to survive a life without credit cards

The thought of living without credit cards was quite worry-some before I took the plunge, but 2 years in — i'm still alive, contributing to society, eating and paying bills, but now with cash, and I feel great. Here's a couple tips i've learned on surviving without credit.

First, set a goal to have a starter emergency fund of atleast $1,000. Using credit cards when its an emergency is the absolute worst time to use a credit card because you're already not thinking clearly and the decisions you make will have financial implications for years to come. For example, my french bulldog recently had an emergency which ended up costing me nearly $13,000.

The old me would have dropped my amex and went on a payment plan for 36 months. The new me, realizing credit cards are inhibitors, not enablers to wealth creation, built an emergency fund...for emergencies.

I used my emergency fund to pay for the $13,000 bill. You should have an emergency fund, it doesn't need to be $13,000 but it needs to be big enough to give you a sense of comfort as you a take leap to life without credit. The feeling I had when paying cash for an emergency and not having to ask myself '" how am I going to pay this off?", is amazing.

What about renting cars or staying at a hotel? This is probably the lamest excuse i've heard from all of my friends and colleagues. You can rent a car using your VISA/MC debit card, and you can also use your debit card to stay at a hotel I know this because between July and December i've rented a car from hertz, and stayed marriott/SPG hotels approximately 16 times (I travel for work). All of which gladly accepted my debit card. The only implication is that Hertz, Marriott and others will put a cash hold on your debit card depending on the duration of the rental. For me, it was anywhere between $60 and $600 dollars.

Did I die? No. Because I have an emergency fund and follow zero-based-budgeting (post on that soon) to plan my expenses for the month ahead.

> *"But John, the hotel put a $600 hold on my debit card!!*
> *I can't afford that"*

The cold truth is that if you can't afford a $600 debit hold for a hotel, you can't afford stay at that hotel or go on vacation. This leads to the next point:

Pay with cash. I've actually embraced the philosophy of envelope-based budgeting where all of my discretionary spending is allocated into a system of 3 envelopes.

1. My fun money.
2. Groceries.
3. Restaurants.

I allocate a % of my post-tax income into those 3 envelopes, and when I run out of money in that envelope — I stop spending money. Crazy isn't it?

All automatic/recurring bills (mortgage, utilities, etc) remain as an auto-expense from my bank account. This process has made me more aware of my spending patterns, and the net result is that I spend approximately 30–50% less on discretionary activities when using cash vs credit. We will cover discretionary spending and income allocation in our chapter on budgeting.

Conclusion: Close all of your credit cards now and forever.

Do you think you can live a life without credit cards? Make a conscious decision and leave the credit rat-race, your FICO score isn't worth it. You've now seen the data, what really happens to your credit score when you close it. I challenge you to embrace a life without credit card debt, a life of living within in your means, a life of spending less than what you make, and a life of freedom — by saying no to credit cards.

SHOULD YOU PAY OFF STUDENT LOANS BEFORE YOU CONTRIBUTE TO YOUR 401K?

You can do two things at once, but you can't focus effectively on two things at once. - Gary Keller

You've recently graduated (or maybe you've been out of school for a while) and everyone — your friends, family, your broke uncle Tom and financial experts across the land all echo the same message:

1. Start contributing to your 401k immediately!

2. Compound interest is king!
3. Your employer's match is free money!

So, following conventional wisdom, we begin contributing to our 401k, usually up to the employer's match, while making concurrent payments towards our student loan. It's definitely what I did when I was younger. Fast forward 8 years later and life kicks our ass: 68% of Americans have an underfunded 401k, our student loans end up in forebarence, we have a $500 a month car loan, no money in our emergency account, and the only light we see at the end of the tunnel is an oncoming train.

How did we end up like this? We were just following the directions of our friends, family, financial experts and society. We just wanted to take advantage of that employer match!

Pay off your student loan debt first

I preface this analysis by saying paying off your student loans *before* contributing to your 401k will not make you broke as long as you can become debt free in < 36 months. There is a direct inverse relationship between you start contributing to your 401k and when you retire. The later in life you start contributing will mean less time you will have to take advantage of "compound interest", and ultimately result in a lower retirement portfolio value.

I'm going to show you that if you can become debt free in < 36 months, then paying off your student loans *before* contributing to your 401k will not cause you to lose out on wealth creation opportunities. If you take 36 months, 48 months, or beyond, you will see a drastic negative impact in the ballpark of $500,000 to over $1,000,000. Don't worry, we will go through this in detail.

Let's take a look at one example, Go-getter Steve:

Go-getter Steve's Profile	
Age	35
Gross Income	$100,000
Student Loan Debt	$66,000
Student Loan Interest	6.00%
Federal Tax Rate	35.00%
401k Contribution	15.00%
401k Employer Match	6.00%
401k Annual Growth	10.00%
Annual Salary increase	5.00%

The profile of Go-getter Steve isn't as uncommon as you think. Steve is 35 years old, he's been out of college for 5 to 8 years, has a household income of $100,000 (combined) but has an aggregate student loan balance of almost $66,000 at 6%. He has a really awesome 401k plan with his employer that matches 100% of the first 6%. He's crushing it at work, averaging a 5% annual salary increase, but he also knows that his household income will never be over $200,000/year, which he's ok with, he knows that in order to make more than $200,000 would mean spending less time with his family. To Steve, more money just isn't worth it. Despite being in the top 5% of income earners, he's late to the retirement game, and at the age of 35 has nothing in his 401k. He wants to fix this by contributing 15% of his post-tax income into a roth 401k while paying his student loan debt down over a 10 year period.

What should Steve do?

Steve really has 2 options:

Option 1 - Contribute to his 401k while paying off student loans.
Option 2 - Pay off student loans first then contribute to his 401k.

Society and conventional wisdom says Steve should contribute to the 401k now and deal with the student loan debt well into his 40s. A lifetime of student loan debt? That sounds *horrible*. We can see that taking the time to conduct an analysis of the two options proves the net impact to Steve's retirement portfolio is negligible. Because there is no impact to Steve's final portfolio, Steve (and most Americans) should proceed with option 2 and pay off the student loan balance before investing his 401k.

Option 1 vs Option 2 Comparison		
	Option 1	Option 2
Roth 401k	$5,343,662.72	$1,297,392.42
Personal Portfolio	$618,704.99	$4,222,199.97
Total	$5,962,367.71	$5,519,592.39

Year over year breakdown of option 1 vs option 2 total portfolio value:

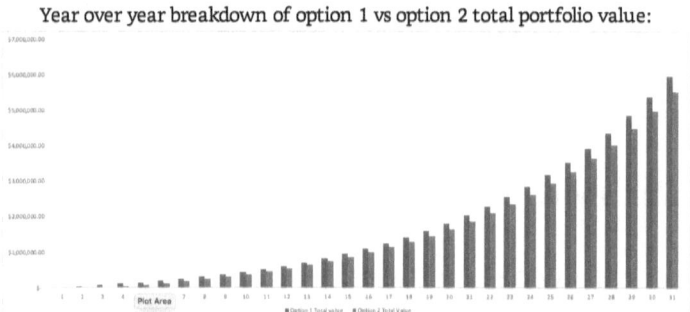

Option 1 in detail:

Let's say Steve follows conventional wisdom and decides to pay his $66,000 loan off in 10 years. He'll pay $732 a month, or $8,788 a year for a total payoff to Uncle Sam of $87,928 — ouch.

Steve is contributing 15% of his income, and his employer is matching 100% of the 1st 6% over this same 10 year period.

Steve contributes $15,000 to $19,000 of his post-tax dollars to his 401k each year, while his employer contributes $6,000 to $9,500. His 401k is growing at an average of 10%. At the end of year 10 he will have approximately $432,000 in his 401k and his student loan will be paid in full. Steve needs to have money and live his life over this same 10 year period, so we've made sure that Steve's free-cash-flow for non-student-loan bills is no lower than 63%. This leaves him with a minimum of $40,000 to spend on an annualized basis. Here's a summary of Steve's financial life from year 1 (age 35) to year 10 (age 44):

Years Investing	Age	Pre-Tax	Post-Tax	Free Cash	Free Cash %	401k Contribution	Employer Match	Student Loan Payment	Personal Portfolio Contribution	401k Value	Personal Portfolio Value	Total Value
1	35	$100,000.00	$65,000.00	$42,250.00	65.00%	$15,000.00	$6,000.00	$8,788.08	$ -	$23,100.00	$ -	$23,100.00
2	36	$109,000.00	$68,750.00	$44,703.75	65.50%	$15,750.00	$6,300.00	$8,788.08	$ -	$49,665.00	$ -	$49,665.00
3	37	$110,250.00	$71,662.50	$47,287.25	66.00%	$16,537.50	$6,615.00	$8,788.08	$ -	$80,099.25	$ -	$80,099.25
4	38	$115,762.50	$75,245.63	$50,038.34	66.50%	$17,364.38	$6,945.75	$8,788.08	$ -	$114,850.31	$ -	$114,850.31
5	39	$121,550.63	$79,007.91	$52,935.30	67.00%	$18,232.59	$7,293.04	$8,788.08	$ -	$154,413.54	$ -	$154,413.54
6	40	$127,628.16	$82,958.30	$55,998.85	67.50%	$19,000.00	$7,657.69	$8,788.08	$ -	$199,178.35	$ -	$199,178.35
7	41	$134,009.56	$87,106.22	$59,232.23	68.00%	$19,000.00	$8,040.57	$8,788.08	$ -	$248,940.82	$ -	$248,940.82
8	42	$140,710.04	$91,461.53	$62,651.15	68.50%	$19,000.00	$8,442.60	$8,788.08	$ -	$303,911.76	$ -	$303,911.76
9	43	$147,745.54	$96,034.60	$66,263.88	69.00%	$19,000.00	$8,864.73	$8,788.08	$ -	$364,954.14	$ -	$364,954.14
10	44	$155,132.82	$100,836.33	$70,081.25	69.50%	$19,000.00	$9,307.97	$8,788.08	$ -	$432,588.32	$ -	$432,588.32

When Steve enters year 11 of investing, he's now 45. Steve is a smart guy, with almost $500k in retirement, he wants to grow his wealth. He takes the $8,788 of now free-cash-flow from his student loans and begins to contribute to a personal investment portfolio outside of his 401k, which is also earning 10% on an annaualized basis. In our table, this is represented by moving the "$8,788.08" from the "Student Loan Payment" column to the "Personal Portfolio Contribution" column He can't contribute the $8,788 to his 401k because he's already maxed out at the $19,000 IRS imposed contribution limit. By the age of 50 Steve achieves his life-long dream of earning $200,000 annually, where he remains until he retires at the age of 65. His net worth at the age of 65? Almost $6 million dollars. He has achieved the American dream of becoming a one percenter and is able to take a portion of his distribution tax free since his retirement vehicle is a roth 401k. Way to go Steve!

Option 1 Retirement Profile: Go-getter Steve	
Age	65
Retirement Portfolio value	$ 5,962,367.71
Annual Distribution	$ 496,863.98
Monthly Distribution	$ 41,405.33

Years Investing	Age	Pre-Tax	Post-Tax	Free Cash	Free Cash %	401k Contribution	Employer Match	Student Loan Payment	Personal Portfolio Contribution	401k Value	Personal Portfolio Value	Total Value
1	35	$100,000.00	$69,000.00	$42,250.00	69.00%	15,000.00	6,000.00	8,788.08		$ 23,100.00		$ 23,100.00
2	36	$109,000.00	$68,250.00	$44,703.75	69.00%	15,750.00	6,300.00	8,788.08		$ 49,665.00		$ 49,665.00
3	37	$110,250.00	$71,662.50	$47,297.25	66.00%	16,537.50	6,615.00	8,788.08		$ 80,099.25		$ 80,099.25
4	38	$118,762.50	$75,245.65	$50,058.84	66.50%	17,364.38	6,945.75	8,788.08		$ 114,850.31		$ 114,850.31
5	39	$121,550.63	$79,007.91	$52,935.30	67.00%	18,232.59	7,293.04	8,788.08		$ 154,413.54		$ 154,413.54
6	40	$127,628.16	$82,958.30	$55,986.85	67.50%	19,000.00	7,657.69	8,788.08		$ 199,178.35		$ 199,178.35
7	41	$134,009.56	$87,106.22	$59,232.29	68.00%	19,000.00	8,040.57	8,788.08		$ 248,840.82		$ 248,840.82
8	42	$140,710.04	$91,461.53	$62,651.13	68.50%	19,000.00	8,442.60	8,788.08		$ 303,811.76		$ 303,811.76
9	43	$147,745.54	$96,034.60	$66,293.88	69.00%	19,000.00	8,864.73	8,788.08		$ 364,834.14		$ 364,834.14
10	44	$155,132.82	$100,836.33	$70,081.29	69.50%	19,000.00	9,307.97	8,788.08		$ 432,388.32		$ 432,388.32
11	45	$163,889.46	$109,878.15	$74,114.71	70.00%	19,000.00	9,773.37		$ 8,788.08	$ 507,457.86	$ 9,666.89	$ 517,164.75
12	46	$171,033.94	$111,172.06	$78,376.30	70.50%	19,000.00	10,262.04		$ 8,788.08	$ 590,435.89	$ 20,300.66	$ 610,736.35
13	47	$179,585.63	$116,730.66	$82,878.77	71.00%	19,000.00	10,775.14		$ 8,788.08	$ 682,232.13	$ 31,997.60	$ 714,229.53
14	48	$188,564.91	$122,567.19	$87,635.54	71.50%	19,000.00	11,313.89		$ 8,788.08	$ 783,800.62	$ 44,864.03	$ 828,664.65
15	49	$197,993.16	$128,695.55	$92,660.80	73.00%	19,000.00	11,879.59		$ 8,788.08	$ 896,148.23	$ 59,017.32	$ 955,165.55
16	50	$200,000.00	$130,000.00	$93,600.00	72.00%	19,000.00	12,000.00		$ 8,788.08	$ 1,019,863.06	$ 74,585.94	$ 1,094,449.00
17	51	$200,000.00	$130,000.00	$93,600.00	72.00%	19,000.00	12,000.00		$ 8,788.08	$ 1,155,049.36	$ 91,713.42	$ 1,247,660.78
18	52	$200,000.00	$130,000.00	$93,600.00	72.00%	19,000.00	12,000.00		$ 8,788.08	$ 1,300,644.30	$ 110,549.65	$ 1,416,193.75
19	53	$200,000.00	$130,000.00	$93,600.00	72.00%	19,000.00	12,000.00		$ 8,788.08	$ 1,470,308.73	$ 131,271.28	$ 1,601,580.01
20	54	$200,000.00	$130,000.00	$93,600.00	72.00%	19,000.00	12,000.00		$ 8,788.08	$ 1,651,439.60	$ 154,065.30	$ 1,805,504.90
21	55	$200,000.00	$130,000.00	$93,600.00	72.00%	19,000.00	12,000.00		$ 8,788.08	$ 1,850,683.56	$ 179,138.72	$ 2,029,822.28
22	56	$200,000.00	$130,000.00	$93,600.00	72.00%	19,000.00	12,000.00		$ 8,788.08	$ 2,069,831.93	$ 206,719.48	$ 2,276,571.40
23	57	$200,000.00	$130,000.00	$93,600.00	72.00%	19,000.00	12,000.00		$ 8,788.08	$ 2,310,837.11	$ 237,058.31	$ 2,547,995.42
24	58	$200,000.00	$130,000.00	$93,600.00	72.00%	19,000.00	12,000.00		$ 8,788.08	$ 2,575,130.82	$ 270,431.03	$ 2,846,561.85
25	59	$200,000.00	$130,000.00	$93,600.00	72.00%	19,000.00	12,000.00		$ 8,788.08	$ 2,867,843.91	$ 307,143.02	$ 3,174,984.93
26	60	$200,000.00	$130,000.00	$93,600.00	72.00%	19,000.00	12,000.00		$ 8,788.08	$ 3,188,728.30	$ 347,522.01	$ 3,536,250.31
27	61	$200,000.00	$130,000.00	$93,600.00	72.00%	19,000.00	12,000.00		$ 8,788.08	$ 3,541,701.13	$ 391,941.10	$ 3,933,642.23
28	62	$200,000.00	$130,000.00	$93,600.00	72.00%	19,000.00	12,000.00		$ 8,788.08	$ 3,929,971.24	$ 440,802.10	$ 4,370,773.34
29	63	$200,000.00	$130,000.00	$93,600.00	72.00%	19,000.00	12,000.00		$ 8,788.08	$ 4,357,068.36	$ 494,549.20	$ 4,851,617.56
30	64	$200,000.00	$130,000.00	$93,600.00	72.00%	19,000.00	12,000.00		$ 8,788.08	$ 4,826,875.20	$ 553,671.01	$ 5,380,546.20
31	65	$200,000.00	$130,000.00	$93,600.00	72.00%	19,000.00	12,000.00		$ 8,788.08	$ 5,343,662.72	$ 618,704.99	$ 5,962,367.71

Option 2 - In detail

Steve can achieve the exact same financial outcome and be debt free in 3 years instead of 10. What if instead of contributing to his 401k, he allocated the same percentage of his free cash flow to paying out his student loan debt? To achieve this, Steve will need to allocate ~$2000/month or ~$24,000 to principal + interest reduction for 36 consecutive months. Over this 36 month period, he isn't contributing to his 401k and he's not receiving any employer contribution. By focusing on just his student loans, he is able to pay off the loan balance in just 30% of the time and save nearly $15,000 in interest. That's $15,000 the US Government won't have to misappropriate!

Save $15,000 by paying your student loans early		
	Option 1	Option 2
Total Principal Paid	$66,000	$66,000
Total Interest Paid	$21,928	$6,283
Total Amount Paid	$87,928	$72,283

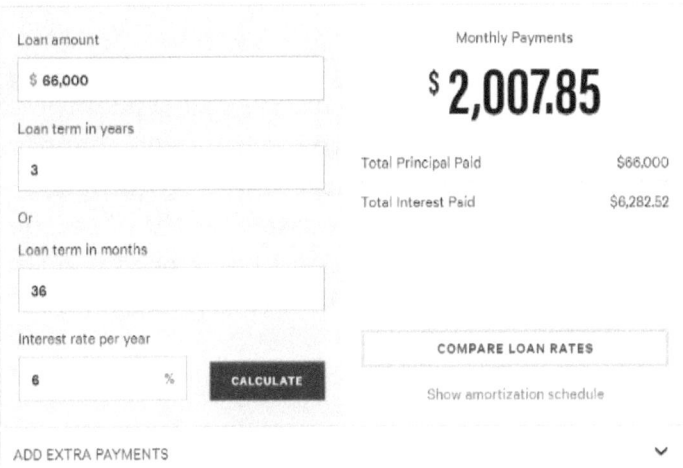

The first 3 years for Go-getter Steve look bleak.

By not contributing to his 401k, not receiving an employer match and not putting any money away for other savings/investing activities, his net worth hovers anywhere between -$66,000 and $0 dollars. Steve perseveres, at and the end of year 3 has had paid a total of $72,000 in student loan and is debt free. He is one of the elite, less than 2 out of 10 Americans are debt free.

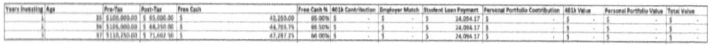

As Steve enters year 4, debt free with over $25,000 to contribute to wealth creation, he maxes out his roth 401k by contributing $19,000 and creates a personal investment portfolio to invest the $8,788 originally earmarked for student loans. Steve achieves career success and earns a household income of $200,000 at age 50 where he remains until retirement. His net worth at the age of 65? Also almost $5.5 million dollars. Steve went against conventional wisdom, paid off his student loan early, paid less in interest to the US government and achieved the American dream of becoming a one percenter ! He receives the same benefit of taking a portion of his distribution tax free since his retirement vehicle is a roth 401k. Way to go Steve!

Option 2 Retirement Profile: Go-getter Steve	
Age	65
Retirement Portfolio value	$5,519,592.39
Annual Distribution	$ 459,966.03
Monthly Distribution	$ 38,330.50

Years Investing	Option 1 - Portfolio Value	Option 2 - Portfolio Value
1	$ 23,100.00	$ -
2	$ 49,665.00	$ -
3	$ 80,099.25	$ -
4	$ 114,850.31	$ 38,207.21
5	$ 154,413.54	$ 80,617.16
6	$ 199,178.35	$ 127,669.23
7	$ 248,840.82	$ 179,847.67
8	$ 303,911.76	$ 237,686.19
9	$ 364,954.14	$ 301,772.90
10	$ 432,588.32	$ 372,755.84
11	$ 517,164.75	$ 451,349.02
12	$ 610,736.35	$ 538,339.05
13	$ 714,229.53	$ 634,592.49
14	$ 828,664.65	$ 741,063.91
15	$ 955,165.55	$ 858,804.74
16	$ 1,094,449.00	$ 988,452.11
17	$ 1,247,660.78	$ 1,131,064.20
18	$ 1,416,193.75	$ 1,287,937.51
19	$ 1,601,580.01	$ 1,460,498.15
20	$ 1,805,504.90	$ 1,650,314.85
21	$ 2,029,822.28	$ 1,859,113.23
22	$ 2,276,571.40	$ 2,088,791.44
23	$ 2,547,995.42	$ 2,341,437.47
24	$ 2,846,561.85	$ 2,619,348.11
25	$ 3,174,984.93	$ 2,925,049.80
26	$ 3,536,250.31	$ 3,261,321.67
27	$ 3,933,642.23	$ 3,631,220.73
28	$ 4,370,773.34	$ 4,038,109.69
29	$ 4,851,617.56	$ 4,485,687.55
30	$ 5,380,546.20	$ 4,978,023.19
31	$ 5,962,367.71	$ 5,519,592.39

Note how Steve is able to compensate for 36 missed months of not contributing to his Roth 401k by getting a 7 year head start on contributing to his personal portfolio, which, by age 65, is $1.2 millon dollars. If Steve followed option 1, his personal non-roth-401k portfolio would have $618,000.

What really matters is at the end of the day, when put all of your money into one big pile, which option produces the biggest pile of money?

All things equal, the total portfolio value of Option 1 is approximately $500,000 greater than the total portfolio value of option 2. This represents an approximate 6% difference or said another way, if you were to take monthly distributions at the age of 65, option 1 would provide around $41,105 of monthly retirement cashflow while option 2 would provide around $38,330 of monthly retirement cashflow.

But what if it took Steve longer than 36 months to pay off his student loan debt?

This is where the value of time and compound interest starts to work against you, and it is also the reason why your student loan debt payoff journey should be a priority. Let's introduce 3 other options (for a total of 5 options):

Option 1 - Make minimum monthly payments and pay off student loans in 10 years while contributing to 401k
Option 2 - Pay off student loans in 36 months & no 401k contribution
Option 3 - Pay off student loans in 48 months & no 401k contribution
Option 4 - Pay off student loans in 60 months & no 401k contribution
Option 5 - Pay off student loans in 72 months & no 401k contribution

The longer Steve waits to pay off his student loan

debt while simulanteously delaying the start of his retirement will cost him over $1,000,000 as outlined below.

Years Investing	Option 1 - Portfolio Value	Option 2 - Portfolio Value	Option 3 - Portfolio Value	Option 4 - Portfolio Value	Option 5- Portfolio Value
1	$ 23,100.00	$ -	$ -	$ -	$ -
2	$ 49,665.00	$ -	$ -	$ -	$ -
3	$ 80,099.25	$ -	$ -	$ -	$ -
4	$ 114,850.31	$ 38,207.21	$ -	$ -	$ -
5	$ 154,413.54	$ 80,617.16	$ 38,589.23	$ -	$ -
6	$ 199,178.35	$ 127,669.23	$ 81,438.50	$ 38,990.35	$ -
7	$ 248,840.82	$ 179,847.67	$ 128,993.87	$ 82,300.90	$ 39,411.52
8	$ 303,911.76	$ 237,686.19	$ 181,747.01	$ 130,384.74	$ 83,206.42
9	$ 364,954.14	$ 301,772.90	$ 240,239.80	$ 183,741.31	$ 131,845.16
10	$ 432,588.32	$ 372,755.84	$ 305,069.43	$ 242,921.09	$ 185,835.33
11	$ 517,164.75	$ 451,349.02	$ 376,893.97	$ 308,530.80	$ 245,736.45
12	$ 610,736.35	$ 538,339.05	$ 456,438.49	$ 381,239.00	$ 312,165.23
13	$ 714,229.53	$ 634,592.49	$ 544,501.88	$ 461,782.44	$ 385,801.29
14	$ 828,664.65	$ 741,063.91	$ 641,964.24	$ 550,972.86	$ 467,393.59
15	$ 955,165.55	$ 858,804.74	$ 749,795.11	$ 649,704.58	$ 557,767.39
16	$ 1,094,449.00	$ 988,452.11	$ 868,541.50	$ 758,441.93	$ 657,311.01
17	$ 1,247,660.78	$ 1,131,064.20	$ 999,162.54	$ 878,053.01	$ 766,809.00
18	$ 1,416,193.75	$ 1,287,937.51	$ 1,142,845.68	$ 1,009,625.20	$ 887,256.79
19	$ 1,601,580.01	$ 1,460,498.15	$ 1,300,897.14	$ 1,154,354.61	$ 1,019,749.36
20	$ 1,805,504.90	$ 1,650,314.85	$ 1,474,753.74	$ 1,313,556.96	$ 1,165,491.18
21	$ 2,029,822.28	$ 1,859,113.23	$ 1,665,996.01	$ 1,488,679.54	$ 1,325,807.19
22	$ 2,276,571.40	$ 2,088,791.44	$ 1,876,362.49	$ 1,681,314.38	$ 1,502,154.79
23	$ 2,547,995.42	$ 2,341,437.47	$ 2,107,765.63	$ 1,893,212.71	$ 1,696,137.16
24	$ 2,846,561.85	$ 2,619,348.11	$ 2,362,309.08	$ 2,126,320.87	$ 1,909,517.76
25	$ 3,174,984.93	$ 2,925,049.80	$ 2,642,306.88	$ 2,382,697.84	$ 2,144,236.43
26	$ 3,536,250.31	$ 3,261,321.67	$ 2,950,304.45	$ 2,664,734.51	$ 2,402,426.96
27	$ 3,933,642.23	$ 3,631,220.73	$ 3,289,101.79	$ 2,974,974.85	$ 2,686,436.54
28	$ 4,370,773.34	$ 4,038,109.69	$ 3,661,778.85	$ 3,316,239.23	$ 2,998,847.09
29	$ 4,851,617.56	$ 4,485,687.55	$ 4,071,723.63	$ 3,691,630.04	$ 3,342,498.68
30	$ 5,380,546.20	$ 4,978,023.19	$ 4,522,662.88	$ 4,104,559.93	$ 3,720,515.44
31	$ 5,962,367.71	$ 5,519,592.39	$ 5,018,596.05	$ 4,558,782.81	$ 4,136,333.87

Steve is not intentional or not 100% committed to paying off his student loan debt as early as possible, then he would be better suited to start contributing to his 401k now as opposed to waiting. If Steve is committed to living a life debt free, than there is no tangible impact from waiting up to 36 months before he starts contributing.

This is why the debate with respecting to "contributing to your 401k now vs later" isn't as clear cut as other financial concepts, e.g. stop using your credit cards. Delaying your contributions to your 401k to pay off your student loan debt early **only works if you are committed.** During my $170,000 student loan debt pay off journey I decided to delay contributing to my 401k because I knew the debt would be paid off in < 24 months. When you calculate your debt pay off timeline, how long will it take you? Are you being as aggressive as possible?

Conclusion: Stop contributing to your 401k if you can pay off your student loan debt in < 36 months.

Most of us try to multi-task and work towards retirement, wealth creation, debt elimination, vacations, and fun money all at the same time. We try to pay on our debt, save a little for emergencies, and contribute the minimum to our 401ks — all from the same paycheck. Not only does this slow our progress of completing a single goal, but it also leaves us unprepared when unexpected expenses arise. Don't get me wrong, Just because contributing to your 401k comes after paying off debt, doesn't mean you should take your time getting to it. You have to move fast, in less than 36 months. The more time you have to save for retirement, the more wealth you can build. So should you stop contributing to your 401k to pay off your student loan? At a minimum, the answer is not an automatic no. You shouldn't do something just because someone, me, your best friend, your broke uncle Tom, tells you to. You need to run the calculations and decide what is the best choice. For me? I've stopped contributing to my 401k during the 15 months it took me to pay off my $170,000 in student loan debt, and I have zero regrets.

PAY AS LITTLE AS POSSIBLE BY REFINANCING YOUR STUDENT LOANS

I'd rather go to bed without dinner than to rise in debt. - Benjamin Franklin

◆ ◆ ◆

Refinancing your student loans is the act of another lender or bank taking ownership of your existing student loans. Technically the new lender pay off the old lender's balance in full, issues a new loan to you (the borrower) at a lower interest rate. You then remit payments to the new lender until the student loan balance is paid in full. The primary reason people do this is to save money on their interest rate. A lower interest rate means a lower monthly payment, which means more cash flow to the borrower. This idea kind of makes sense if you're planning on grinding out a student loan repayment plan in excess of 5, 10 or 15 years.

The interest rate on my student loans hovered between 5.31% and 7.00% and although didn't think refinancing my student loans to a lower interest rate would net a meaningful impact since (since my goal was to pay it off in < 24 months),

 I decided to run the numbers to quantify potential savings of refinancing on refinancing $145,000 of debt. When you're exploring the possiblity of refinancing it's important to quantify not only the interest rate savings but your total time horizon to see if going through the gyrations & pile of paperwork is really worth it.

Here's how to determine if you should refinance your student loans.

First determine your time horizon to being debt

free. Will it take you six months or 36 months? I set an incredibly aggressive goal of paying off $145,000 between 8 and 12 months. Once you've determined your time horizon, the next step is to determine how much student loan interest you'll pay in that time frame. If i assume the lower end of 8 months to being debt free, I would pay approximately $6,084 of interest. Here's how:

Total amount of interest = (Current interest rate / 365) * (# of days in 8 months) * outstanding loan balance.

If I plug in my numbers to that formula I get a value of "total amount of interest" = $6084.71. My average interest rate across my student loans is approximately 6.32% (or .0632). Total amount of interest = (.0632/365)*(241)*145813.80. Here's a table of the results, be sure to perform this calculation on your student loan debt before proceeding.

Current Interest Rate	6.32000%
Daily Interest Rate	0.01732%
Number of days in 8 months	241
Outstanding loan balance	$ 145,813.80
Interest Paid	$ 6,084.71

The thought of giving ANY money to the US government makes me cringe. So I thought to myself, is there any way I can limit the amount of cash I pay to these incompetent bureaucrats while continuing to meet my debt obligations? The answer is yes. There are many commercial lenders which offer the opportunity to pay a lower interest rate than what's available via the US Department of Education and it's current subsidized/unsubsidized loan programs, which charge SEVEN PERCENT! Yikes! Here i've compared student loan refinancing options from 4 major lenders:

1. SoFi: 4.324%
2. Earnest: 3.790%
3. Commonboard: 3.890%
4. Laurel Road: 4.250%

So we can see that Earnest offered me the lowest rate. 3.790% to consolidate $145,000 with a blended rate of 6.32%. They also sent me this funny email letting me know I was in the 'top 3% of applicants'. Like, ok? Is this supposed to be a compliment? I'm in $145,000 of student loan debt! The question remains, is this refinancing activity actually going to save me any MONEY?! I ran the cost projections for each of the 4 lenders, with a 12 month and 8-month repayment window and here are the summary results.

Lending Institution	Annual Rate	Interest Paid in 12 months	Interest Paid in 8 months	12 Months Savings
Current Lender	6.32%	$ 9,215.43	$ 6,084.71	$ -
SoFi	4.32%	$ 6,304.99	$ 4,163.02	$ 2,910.44
Earnest	3.79%	$ 5,526.34	$ 3,648.90	$ 3,689.09
Commonboard	3.89%	$ 5,672.16	$ 3,745.18	$ 3,543.28
Laurel Rate	4.25%	$ 6,197.09	$ 4,091.77	$ 3,018.35

Column 1 is the lender, column 2 is the annual interest rate, column 3 is estimated interest paid at 12 months, column 4 is estimated interest paid at 8 months, and column 5 is amount saved in 12 months by refinancing to another lender. The net result is that I can save around $3,689 by refinancing to Earnest. Which is slightly north of $300/month. Certainly compelling. The details to derive the summary table above can be found below. If you're thinking about refinancing your student loans, it is definitely a worthwhile activity to perform this exercise on your own so you can actually quantify your projected savings.

		Current - 6.32%		SoFi, 4.324%		Earnest - 3.79%		Commonboard - 3.89%		Laurel Road - 4.25%	
Outstanding Balance	Annual Interest Rate	12 months	8 months	12 months	8 months	12 months	8 months	12 months	8 months	12 months	8 months
$ 2,915.51	6.31%	$ 184.26	$ 122.67	$ 126.07	$ 83.93	$ 110.50	$ 73.56	$ 113.41	$ 75.51	$ 123.91	$ 82.49
$ 22,196.01	5.31%	$ 1,402.79	$ 933.91	$ 959.76	$ 638.96	$ 841.23	$ 560.05	$ 863.42	$ 574.83	$ 943.33	$ 628.03
$ 38,064.64	6.31%	$ 2,405.60	$ 1,601.59	$ 1,645.92	$ 1,095.77	$ 1,442.65	$ 960.45	$ 1,480.71	$ 985.79	$ 1,617.75	$ 1,077.02
$ 37,900.64	7.00%	$ 2,395.32	$ 1,594.69	$ 1,638.82	$ 1,091.05	$ 1,436.45	$ 956.31	$ 1,474.33	$ 981.54	$ 1,610.78	$ 1,072.38
$ 23,425.85	7.00%	$ 1,480.51	$ 985.66	$ 1,012.93	$ 674.36	$ 887.84	$ 591.08	$ 911.27	$ 606.68	$ 995.60	$ 662.82
$ 25,291.34	7.00%	$ 1,598.41	$ 1,064.15	$ 1,093.60	$ 728.07	$ 958.54	$ 638.15	$ 983.83	$ 654.99	$ 1,074.88	$ 715.61
$ 149,793.99		$ 9,466.98	$ 6,302.67	$ 6,477.09	$ 4,312.15	$ 5,677.19	$ 3,779.61	$ 5,826.99	$ 3,879.34	$ 6,366.24	$ 4,238.35

Keep in mind if you refi to any private lender, you lose certain 'perks' of the existing US Department of Education's loan program such as income-based repayment. If you plan on taking 10 or 15 years to pay off your student loans, this is something you should consider. But then again, you shouldn't take 10 years, 5 years, or even 3 years to pay off your student loans. They're handcuffs of the middle class which will prevent you from achieving economic wealth creation.

Fast forward six months

At the $145,000 mark with the interest rate options provided I made a decision to not proceed with refinancing until I hit sub $100,000. Which I achieved in December 2019. Using earnest as the prevailing lender I re-appied with approximately $98,179.79 and was approved for a 3.45% interest rate, pictured below.

Say hello to your new Earnest loan.

Now that you have the Earnest loan that you deserve, we're here to help guide you through repayment. As your servicer, we will get you answers to your questions, provide resources, and celebrate each milestone you achieve - bringing you closer to financial success.

Your loan summary
Current balance: $98,179.79
Current interest rate: 3.450%
Lender: EARNEST OPERATIONS LLC

Manage your online account
Visit earnest.com to enjoy convenient access to your account information, make payments, and manage your eDelivery and Auto Pay enrollment. You may even be eligible for a .25% interest rate reduction with Auto Pay! (See important disclosure section.)

Keep an eye out for your first billing statement
It will arrive soon and includes your new Monthly Payment Amount and due date *(hint: you can always call us to change your due date).*

Quick back napkin math to see how much interest I'd be able to save if I were able to re-finance my ~7% federal subsidized/unsubsidized loans to a rate < 4%.

	Current	Earnest
Loan Balance	$ 98,179.79	$ 98,179.79
Interest Rate	7.000%	3.750%
Interest Paid	$ 6,872.59	$ 3,681.74
Total Amount Paid	$ 105,052.38	$ 101,861.53
Potential savings		$ 3,190.84

On an annualized basis, not taking into account any principal reduction, I would save somewhere in the neighborhood of $3,000; see table. If you are considering refinancing your student loans to a lower interest rate, it is critical you perform these calculations prior to making a go/no-go decision.

Keep in my mind I have no desire let this debt linger and this refi activity would save at MOST $3,000. But hey, if someone gave me $3,000, I would take it. After a quick reapplication via earnest which included uploading my proof of income and assets, I received a *fantastic* (sarcasm) email with the title "Say Hello to your new earnest loan".

Within 15 days, Earnest sent payment in full to original lender (The US Department of Education), and just like that...I have a new master...I mean lender. So are you thinking about refinancing your student loans? Ok i'll bite..go ahead and give it a try, but under no circumstance should you convince yourself that you've actually accomplished anything. Because you haven't. You're still broke. There's only one way out of debt, and that's by aggressively paying it off!

Conclusion: Refinance your student loans to a

lower rate to save money, but continue to pay the debt as quickly as possible.

THE GOVERNMENT WILL NOT FORGIVE YOUR DEBT

Give a man an education and he will build a new world but give a man a loan and you can own that man forever. - Unknown

It should be no surprise to anyone but in the event it's not crystal clear: The US Department Federal Student Loan program is an absolute failure. It is a social experiment gone wrong and now serves as another expense to American taxpayers. The Congressional Budget Office, a government agency which provides budget and economic information to Congress, has concluded that America's student loan program will now cost taxpayers $31 billion dollars over the next 10 years. This adds insult to injury because in 2013, the CBO estimated the program would yield $184 billion dollars in profit for the US Government.

The incompetency of the US Department of Education

Imagine if this were a corporate enterprise and in a 5-year window revenue swung from $184B in profit to $31B in losses? Rational minds would prevail and the entity would be forced in bankruptcy, liquidation and a more efficient firm would enter the market and serve the gap left from the defunct firm. But rational minds don't exist within the US Government and certainly not within the disaster known as the US Department of Education. Why is the federal loan program now posting a $31B loss?

How do we explain this insanity? The answer is simple, but accepting it is hard: We (American taxpayers) are giving 18-year-olds a BLANK check to attend college and major in left-handed puppetry. This is our fault because our federal banking system and its lenders would never lend $20,000, $40,000 or $100,000 to an 18-year-old. So how do we respond? By guaranteeing loan repayment to lenders. Let that sink in, the banks *know* these 18-year-olds have a high probability of default and in an open market, wouldn't lend a penny to them. The US Department of Education has to guarantee (promise) that if/when these 18-year-olds fail, taxpayers will step in and save them.

When American taxpayers guarantee student loans, tuition skyrockets. Why does tuition skyrocket? By providing unlimited capital to college students for tuition, colleges are able to command an unlimited amount for tuition. The barrier to entry for an 18-year-old to obtain a $50,000 student loan is an "online exam" which takes 30 minutes to complete. It takes more work to get a car loan than it does a student loan. The net result? College tuition which rises at 12x the rate of inflation. Madness.

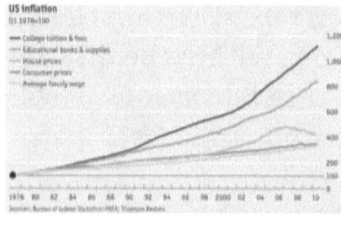

The PLUS loan program's interest rate will reach an estimated 8.35% with a max cap of 10.50%. This means that for every 100 dollar student loan payment you make to the Department of Education, 10 dollars will be allocated to interest. In addition to the insanity of the increased interest rates, we find that over $3B yearly is allocated toward's student loan administration. Think of the incompetent bureaucrats swimming in a sea of mediocrity pushing paper from pile 1 to pile 2. Complete waste of money.

So what exactly are the cogs in the US Department of Education doing with a $3 billion dollar budget?

Doing what they do best, destroying the lives of the middle class. Let's look at the "Public Service Loan Forgiveness" program. This program 'forgives' student loan debt if you meet a specific set of criteria which includes: on-time payment for 120 months, working for a government agency (no thanks), among others. Since it's inception PSLF has received 86,006 applications for forgiveness. Only 864 applications were actually forgiven.

The dismal numbers of the Public Service Loan Forgiveness Program	
Unique Borrowers Submitting PSLF Applications	73,554
Total Number of PSLF Applications	86,006
PSLF Applications Pending Processing	10,004
PSLF Applications with Processing Complete	76,002
Count of PSLF Applications approved by the servicer	864
Total Balance Forgiven	$30,688,445
Average debt per applicant	$35,519.03
% Approved	1.004981%
% Denied	98.995419%

98.9% OF ALL APPLICATIONS FOR FORGIVENESS WERE DENIED. A 3 billion dollar expense set up for the sole purpose of administrating student loans then denying forgiveness based on an irrational set of requirements unattainable to 99% of Americans.

Conclusion: Do not rely on the US Government to forgive your student loan debt, because they will not.

Moreover, cancel the US Department of Education's Federal Student Loan Program. By eliminating the unlimited access to capital, demand (# of people who want to attend ridiculously priced universities) will decrease. When demand decreases, supply (the # of worthless private universities selling liberal arts degrees for $100k) will also decrease. The net result is cheaper tuition. Keep federal programs like the Pell Grant available to help those truly in need and encourage a 2-year community college transfer program for pennies on the dollar.

With the Federal Student Loan Program shut down, we can now address the elephant in the room: the $1.5 trillion dollar student loan debt fiasco. We need to eliminate the failed Student Loan Forgiveness Program and mandate a 33% post-tax automatic deduction against all individuals with an outstanding student loan balance. That means if you make $1,000 a month 33% or $333 will go towards your student loan debt. If you make $10,000 a month $3,333 will go towards your student loan debt. Enforce this plan until all student loan debt obligations paid. Then and only then can we move on from the failed social experiment known as student loans.

CONTROL YOUR MONEY WITH A BUDGET

A debt problem is, at its core, a budgeting problem. - Unknown

At its core, creating a personal budget is telling your money what to do, ideally before the start of the month. How many times have you asked yourself "Where the hell did my money go?", or think to yourself " I thought I had more money in my bank account". Those statements used to run through my mind...often. I thought the answer to this problem was to **make more money.** I thought that by making more money I wouldn't have to worry about where my money went, because I'd have plenty of it! I was wrong. I can't tell you if money buys happiness, but I can tell you that money will make you more of what you already are. Do you spend alot of money? Terrible with managing a budget? Money will only magnify these challenges. Alternatively, if you're great with money, an astute investor, or philanthropist, money will highlight these strengths. My conclusion is that more money alone will not fix poor spending habits. What fixed my spending habits and turned my income into a powerhouse **was a personal budget.**

Specifically, a zero-based personal budget which is a type of income and expense planning approach that allocates every dollar to an expense so that your income — expense = zero. Now, these expenses can be any category you want: fun money, vacation savings, a new dog, the expense category really doesn't matter. The core tenant with a zero-based budget is that every dollar is allocated to an expense category. By the end of this book, you will be liberated with a zero based budget. Although zero-based personal budget planning is a rather mechanical activity where you 'zero out' your income against your personal expense categories, there are 4 pillars which serve as the foundation for a zero-based budget. All 4 pillars operate in unison like 4 legs on a chair, take one leg away and what happens to the chair? It collapses. Follow these 4 steps, and you'll feel like you a got a raise.

Rule 1: Know every expense

It does not matter if you make $1,000 or $100,000, you need to know all of your expenses, yes even the $0.99 Apple iTunes recurring expense. For example, I have $9.93 of itunes storage expense every month. This represents 0.0005969% of an average month's income, but I include it anyway. If you're a little loose with cashflow like I was, this exercise will serve as a good analysis & review all of your digital < $20 subscriptions, which for me, adds up to $54.90 a month. When I first implemented a detail personal budget, I realized that I was spending well over $200 a month in digital subscriptions, and was paying for HBO-go twice. Take the time to review all of your recurring expenses, even the < $20.

Pay Period 1 (1st to 15th)		Pay Period 2(16th to 28th)	
Subscriptions:		Subscriptions:	
iTunes	$5.99	myFitnessPal	$9.99
Spotify	$14.99	The Ready State	$9.99
WSJ	$9.99		

Rule 2: Know the due date of each expense

When I was younger and first started making more than $100k a year, I used alot of 'mental math' to manage my money. Not really knowing the exact due dates of individual bills (e.g. utilities, cable) but justifying it by knowing that regardless if the bill was due on the 3rd or the 20th, I was reasonably confident that I'd have enough cash in the back to cover it. Although this works for many people, it creates a scenario in which it's too easy to lose track of expenses while simultaneously encouraging potentially wreckless spending. To avoid this, put each expenses' due date in the expense line item. This will also ensure you know if it's a bill you're paying on with paycheck 1, or paycheck 3. **Know the exact date each expense is due.**

Rule 3: Every dollar has a budget

Some people call this 'zero-based budgeting', which is a fancy way of taking every dollar of income and mapping to an expense. If you earn $11,324.56 in one month, then you would have $11,324.56 of expenses, not $10,500 or $11,300. An easy way to manage excess income is to allocate additional earnings to a single discretionary category, in my example, the wedding. Your remaining balance (income — expense) should always equal to 0.

Pay Period 1 (1st to 15th)		Pay Period 2 (16th to 28th)	
Income 1	$5,000	Income 1	$5,000
Income 2	$5,000	Income 2	$5,000
Total Income:	$10,000.00	Total Income:	$10,000.00
Total Expense:	$10,000	Total Expense:	$10,000
Amount unbudgeted:	$0.00	Amount unbudgeted:	$0.00

Rule 4: Pay your bills with your debit card

Alot of my friends and peers pay their utilities, groceries, and other living expenses with their credit card and in turn, pay off the credit card at the end of the month. This is primarily done in the pursuit of cash back or reward points. This mental math and additional burden is not worth it. 1% cash would yield just $1,000 if you spend $100,000. Countless studies have shown that you spend more when you pay with credit card vs cash. You are not winning. Furthermore, it's another transaction which needs to be reconciled and zeroed out in your excel/personal finance app of choice. You're also supporting an industry which makes money off the backs of the poor and middle class. No thanks.

Conclusion: Pay with your debit card and avoid the headache.

A BUDGET IN ACTION

*Becoming rich is hard. Staying broke is hard.
Choose your hard. - Eric Worre*

◆ ◆ ◆

This is the moment of truth, the culmination of the ideals and messages conveyed in this book are materialized in this chapter, it's time to budget. The ideal time to create your monthly budget is before the start of the month. As we go through this example, remember that you're planning for the <u>next month</u>. In this example, we'll create a budget for an individual or household who makes $11,000/month post-tax. $10,000 from their "day job", and $1,000 from a "side hustle".

The $11,000 of income is distributed across 5 categories, outlined below. Note how every penny of income in this eaxmple is allocated to a budget category, there is no 'buffer'. More specifically, this budget is telling me that i'll be living off 41.41% of my post tax income. 58.59% of my post tax income, or $6,445.04, will be allocated to student loan debt.

Category	Budget Amount	% of Total
Student Loans:	$6,445.04	58.59%
Housing:	$2,400.00	21.82%
Insurance:	$119.99	1.09%
Digital Subscriptions:	$34.97	0.32%
Life:	$2,000.00	18.18%
Total	**$11,000.00**	**100.00%**

I have a 'budget template' that serves as my starting point, but always end up customizing it for the one-off bills that are due in each particular month. Creating your personal budget is personal and underscores your values, beliefs, hopes and dreams. Despite the uniqueness of our lives, there are 4 core rules that all personal budgets need to follow. There is no exception: **follow these rules and own your money.**

1. **Know every expense**
2. **Know the due date of every expense**
3. **Every dollar has a budget**
4. **Pay your bills with your debit card**

Now that we're aligned on the 4 rules of creating a personal budget, let's dive into the details. Here is a completeed "zero based" budget. The layout of your budget should look like this. The categories may be different, the amounts may be different, but the flow of income to expenses with every dollar allocated to a budget should be a common theme. It should read like a profit & loss or income statement. You are the CFO of You, Inc and you've been hired to manage your income. Remember, plan your budget before the month begins.

Pay Period - 1st to 15th		Pay Period - 16th to 31st	
Category	Amount	Category	Amount
Paycheck 1	$5,000.00	Paycheck 2	$5,000.00
Side Hustle	$500.00	Side Hustle	$500.00
Total Income	**$5,500.00**	**Total Income**	**$5,500.00**
Student Loans:		**Student Loans:**	
Dept of Education (10th)	$4,075.02	Dept of Education (20th)	$2,370.02
Housing:		**Housing:**	
Utilities (3rd)	$200.00	Rent (25th)	$2,000.00
Cell (5th)	$100.00	Internet (20th)	$100.00
Insurance:		**Insurance:**	
Car Insurance (10th)	$100.00	Renter's Insurance (20th)	$19.99
Digital Subscriptions:		**Digital Subscriptions:**	
iTunes (3rd)	$9.99	myFitnessPal (20th)	$9.99
Spotify (5th)	$14.99		
Life:		**Life:**	
Gas	$200.00	Gas	$200.00
Groceries	$400.00	Groceries	$400.00
Restaurant	$200.00	Restaurant	$200.00
Fun Money	$200.00	Fun Money	$200.00
Total Expenses	**$5,500.00**	**Total Expenses**	**$5,500.00**
Remaining:	$0.00	Remaining:	$0.00

Income

The frequency in which you're paid will ultimately determine the # of columns you'll have in your personal budget template. If, for example, I was paid every week, it may be easier for me to have 4 columns and in turn allocate individual expenses to one of the 4 columns. Right now, my income is distributed twice, on the 1st and again on the 16th, so i've created 2 columns to represent this distribution. Column 1 says "I will receive $5,500 on the 1st which will pay for all bills due on the 1st to the 15th". Column 2 says "I will receive $5,500 on the 16th which will pay for all bills due on the 16th to the 31st".

Pay Period - 1st to 15th		Pay Period - 16th to 31st	
Category	Amount	Category	Amount
Paycheck 1	$5,000.00	Paycheck 2	$5,000.00
Side Hustle	$500.00	Side Hustle	$500.00
Total Income	**$5,500.00**	**Total Income**	**$5,500.00**

My expenses will all be allocated into one of the two columns:

1. Column 1 - expenses paid between the 1st and the 15th
2. Column 2 - expenses paid between the 16th and 31st

Student Loans

Student Loans:		Student Loans:	
Dept of Education (10th)	$4,075.02	Dept of Education (20th)	$2,370.02

At a minimum I was required to make a $2,002 monthly payment towards my student loan, due on the 10th. In the spirit of rapidly paying off your student loan debt, all excess income should be placed in this category, as depicted above. This is where you should make your income - expenses = 0. Despite the required minimum payment of $2,002, an extra payment of $4,443.04 will be made for a total of $6445.04. In aggregate this payment is approximately $58.59% of this month's total budget.

Housing

Housing:		Housing:	
Utilities (3rd)	$200.00	Rent (25th)	$2,000.00
Cell (5th)	$100.00	Internet (20th)	$100.00

I categorize housing expenses as anything related to my physical dwelling which includes: utilities, cell phone (I get it, this is negotiable), storage, rent and internet. All of these expenses are recurring, and therefore included in my budget template. Housing represents 21.82% of my total income, of which rent represents 18%. The rent in SF is out of control, but I've took on roommates to reduce expenses and accelerate my student loan debt repayment schedule. Note how expenses are categorized into column 1 or column 2 depending on the due date. This helps manage cashflow and ensure I never reach a negative balance in my checking account.

Insurance

Insurance:		Insurance:	
Car Insurance (10th)	$100.00	Renter's Insurance (20th)	$19.99

The insurance category includes all insurance types with the exception of health insurance. My rationale for excluding health insurance is that although it is paid for with post-tax dollars, it is deducted from my paycheck before deposited into my account. It is possible to make a case to include it in your personal budget, but at the very minimum you should know how much your health insurance costs you on a monthly or annualized basis. If I were to include personal health insurance, it would be an additional $105 per month or $52.50 per pay period. Car and renters insurance are recurring bills which are part of my budget template, but if you have any health or other medical expenses, it may be appropriate to add that expense to this insurance category. This category represents 1.09% of this month's income.

Digital Subscriptions

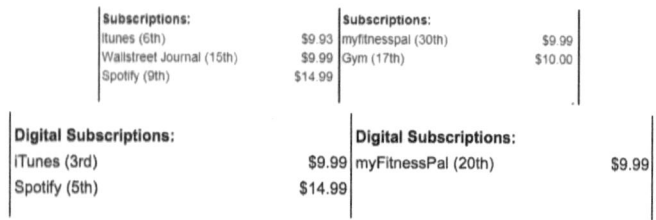

Digital subscriptions represent all of the subscriptions (apps, news) which I pay for a monthly basis. This includes: iTunes, Spotify, and myFitnessPal. In aggregate this is 0.32% of this budget. Although this category is small, it was by far the most difficult for me to quantify when i first started. I actually had no clue how many digital subscriptions I had 1 year ago today. Think about your digital platforms: amazon, facebook, apple, google, hulu, netflix, and so on. Can you quantify the number of digital subscriptions you have right now , the corresponding due dates, and bill amount? If not, take time track down this information. For me, this category was originally > $200 a month 1 year ago today!

Life

Life:		Life:	
Gas	$200.00	Gas	$200.00
Groceries	$400.00	Groceries	$400.00
Restaurant	$200.00	Restaurant	$200.00
Fun Money	$200.00	Fun Money	$200.00

Think of life as my day-to-day expenses which keep me moving. Gas, groceries, restaurants, gym, and fun money. If you're planning a budget for the first time, this will be the hardest category to quantify, and you will most likely under-estimate how much money you spend on groceries and restaurants. It took me almost 3 months to get an accurate measurement on how much money I really spent on food. Once you're able to quantify life expenses, this is the area where you will tighten your belt.

Relative to the % of total, life represents 18.18% this month's budget template, and "fun money" represents only 3.64%. For those in debt, starting a budget for the first time, or not sure where to start. Focus on your 'life' category. It's ok if the individual line items or budget amounts or % of totals dont match mine. What's important is for you to be able to know with confidence how much you're spending on life's necessities.

What about budgeting software?

If you follow this plan, and use excel, there is no need to use software like (YNAB, mint.com, etc). Your money is planned before the month starts, and once you enter the month, you tell your money what to do, not some random app. Most people do not need software to manage a personal budget. I actually withdraw cash twice a month (1st and 16th) to use as my fun money. The quantity of transactions which flow through my checking account are minimal. No software required. There aren't any hacks to personal finance or managing a budget. There isn't a single piece of software which is going to make you financially responsible!

Conclusion:

Personal finance is 80% personal and 20% finance. I like to think that making the budget is the easiest part. Enforcing the budget, agreeing on expense category budgets with your significant other, figuring out how much money you actually spending eat out every month, that's the personal part of personal finance. Don't give up, it took me 3 months to get an accurate picture of how much money I really spent on restaurants and groceries. With my personal finances now under control, the feeling is amazing. It's like I gave myself a raise — for the first time in my life, I was telling my money what to do!

YOUR DEBT FREE PLAN VS REALITY

Pay off your debt first. Freedom from debt is worth more than any amount you can earn. — Mark Cuban

◆ ◆ ◆

July 18th, 2020, 8am pacific standard time. I no longer work at an office, my commute has been reduced from a 1 hour CalTrain ride to a 30 second walk from my bedroom to my home office. I log into my Earnest student loan portal, something that I do every morning, to check the payoff balance of my student loans, originally $170,000. Every login, every day, I cringe a bit, reminded of the poor decisions I made while in school. Reminded of how easy it was to apply for and be approved of over $170,000 of unsubsidized student loans. 100% digital. But on July 18th, 2020, something special happened that day. July 18th, 2020 is a day I will never forget. Because on July 18th, 2020:

I MADE MY LAST STUDENT LOAN PAYMENT AND BECAME 100% DEBT FREE!

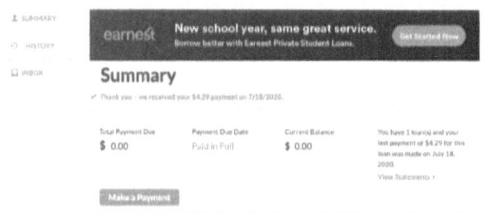

For the first time in my life, for the first time in my wife's life, we became 100% debt free. We owe no one nothing. The borrower is not slave to the lender in my house. The feeling was amazing. When we went to the grocery store on July 18th, 2020, the food tasted better, the sun shined brighter, the insanity of a COVID filled world didn't seem to matter as much, because for the first time in our life, we didn't have to worry about our "monthly debt service".

Together we crushed our credit card debt, cash

flowed a wedding, supported our love ones as they personally suffered (financially, mentally and physically) from COVID19. Those aforementioned events cost us north of $100,000 over a 24 month window. Yet this event was special in its own way, paying off $170,000 seemed untenable given the current economic climate, 15% unemployment rate, $1.3 trillion dollars of outstanding student loan debt, the list goes on and on. But we overcame.

The start.

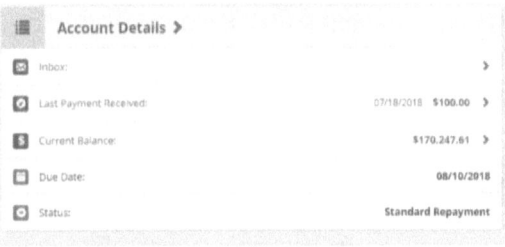

Exactly 24 months ago, after graduating from USC with an MBA, it was finally time to meet my maker; the US Department of Education. After a not so kind 6 month grace period, our first payment became due; $2,002 a month for the next 10 years on a balance of $170,247.61. That's a total repayment amount of over $240,000.

We went through a roller coaster of emotions. First we were apathetic; "whatever" we thought... "this is normal, everyone has student loan debt". Well... "we make enough money, it's not that big of a deal". Then panic set in, the idea of home ownership in the bay area was fleeting, even with a dual income household w/ no kids. Then sadness and depression set in, wishing that we could go back in time and rewind the hands of student loan debt.

But ultimately the end result was ownership. We realized the only way out of debt, is to pay off debt. We cancelled our honeymoon and all vacations. We downsized our living situation and got a roommate. We sold our expensive german-made luxury sedans and got a used 2008 ford focus. More importantly, we agreed that it was time to change our relationship with money. Specifically:

NO CONSUMER DEBT: We decided that there is no scenario where consumer debt (credit cards, car loans, car leases, student loans, etc) would be acceptable. Ever again. We became a 100% pay-with-cash family. When we decided to close all of our credit cards and adhere to a life of cash, it became incredibly freeing. We do not regret it at all, yet we caught alot of grief from others "over the value of credit". My personal opinion is that credit cards are the cigarettes of the financial services industry. Credit cards keep poor people poor, and the middle class from climbing the socioeconomic ladder.

LIVE ON A WRITTEN BUDGET: We committed to living on a written budget where we set a goal to live on 60% of our post tax income. This would enable us to throw around 40% to student loan debt. Re-read the chapters on budgeting if you need a refresher.

BE ALIGNED ON GOALS: Over this 24 month journey there were definitely times where I squeezed the budget a little too hard and tried to live on nothing..literally. Although that may work for a month or two, it caused alot of un-needed grief and tension between my wife and I. It is alot easiser to align on a big macro goal "Pay off student loan debt in X months", and adjust to the interim ebbs and flows. If you make a small mistake along the way, forgive yourself. Our original goal was to pay off $170,000 of student loan debt in 21 months, but we failed.

We were bummed, but candidly some unexpected stuff happened. Family emergencies, career changes, missed bonus pools, COVID etc. All in, it took us 24 months, and we're ok.

The plan vs reality.

I think an upside of this crazy student loan debt pay off journey was building a meaningful relationship with our money. My wife and I meticulously tracked our expenses, by transaction and category, every month. We were able to track our planned pay off date vs our actual. Externally to our friends, family, and the internet, starting on July 2018, we wanted to pay off $170,000 by March 2020. That's about 21 months. Internally, we set an aggressive goal to pay it off by December 2019, that's around 18 months. On both fronts we failed. The table below outlines the details. The columns with the black header represent our "planned" pay-off amount, balance, and date. The columns in blue represent our reality.

Month	Payment	Additional Payment	Total Payment	Projected Interest	Projected Principal	Projected Balance	Actual Payment	Actual Interest	Actual Principal	Actual Balance
Jul-18	$1,510.57	$750.00	$3,210.57	$	478.82	$ 1,833.75	$ 169,724.04	$1,834.75	$1.00	$1,833.75	$168,724.04
Aug-18	1,800.00		1,800.00		584.50	1,015.45	$ 168,708.59	$1,600.00	$584.55	$1,015.45	$168,948.40
Sep-18	2,002.00		2,002.00		236.08	1,765.92	$ 166,942.67	$2,002.00	$236.08	$1,765.92	$167,662.61
Oct-18	2,002.00		2,002.00		19.91	1,982.09	$ 164,960.58	$2,002.00	$19.91	$1,982.09	$166,450.37
Nov-18	2,002.00		2,002.00		945.78	1,056.22	$ 163,904.36	$2,002.00	$851.20	$1,150.80	$165,521.99
Dec-18	2,002.00		2,002.00		939.79	1,062.21	$ 162,842.15	$2,000.02	$1,274.49	$725.53	$164,110.31
Jan-19	2,002.00		2,002.00		933.78	1,068.22	$ 161,773.93	$2,002.00	$231.06	$1,770.94	$162,894.96
Feb-19	2,002.00		2,002.00		927.72	1,074.28	$ 160,699.65	$2,002.48	$891.65	$1,110.84	$161,632.94
Mar-19	2,002.00		2,002.00		921.63	1,080.37	$ 159,619.28	$2,002.00	$825.76	$1,176.24	$160,722.20
Apr-19	2,002.00	$32,696.00	34,698.00		915.51	1,086.49	$ 120,836.79	$14,218.01	$907.90	$13,311.11	$157,650.78
May-19	2,002.00	$11,223.00	13,225.00		909.36	1,092.64	$ 113,521.15	$10,325.98	$893.68	$9,432.30	$142,619.49
Jun-19	2,002.00	$11,223.00	13,225.00		903.15	1,098.84	$ 101,199.31	$2,691.31	$734.38	$1,956.93	$138,361.73
Jul-19	2,002.00	$21,473.00	23,475.00		896.94	1,105.05	$ 78,621.25	$4,118.72	$651.59	$3,467.13	$134,502.24
Aug-19	2,002.00	$11,223.00	13,225.00		890.68	1,111.32	$ 66,286.93	$6,000.06	$802.35	$5,197.71	$127,244.58
Sep-19	2,002.00	$11,223.00	13,225.00		884.38	1,117.62	$ 53,948.31	$13,346.74	$1,225.68	$12,121.06	$118,145.42
Oct-19	2,002.00	$21,473.00	23,475.00		878.04	1,123.98	$ 31,349.35	$16,624.71	$37.45	$16,587.26	$114,650.12
Nov-19	2,002.00	$11,223.00	13,225.00		871.66	1,130.32	$ 19,096.03	$2,176.39	$578.73	$1,597.66	$98,179.70
Dec-19	2,002.00	$17,860.00	19,862.00		865.27	1,136.73	$ (0.76)	$6,993.63	$293.04	$6,700.59	$91,479.20
Jan-20								$6,116.86	$238.10	$5,878.76	$85,707.13
Feb-20								$11,384.00	$104.84	$11,279.46	$74,134.39
Mar-20								$2,000.00	$229.10	$1,770.90	$73,676.74
Apr-20								$16,792.29	$266.55	$16,525.74	$56,151.62
May-20								$7,337.26	$87.22	$7,337.26	$48,917.23
Jun-20								$1,788.19	$82.96	$1,705.23	$47,201.02
Jul-20								$45,580.49	$60.10	$45,520.39	$0.00

Note just how short we were by December 2019. We still had $91,000 of student loan debt to pay off. Looking back on the journey, we made this plan when my wife and I were both in different roles at different organizations. Believe it or not, since July 2018 my wife and I have each changed employers twice. That was something we didn't plan for or expect in 2018. She now runs her own company, and I work at a start up. Unfortunately life events such as 'career changes' weren't factored into the original 18 month pay off window.

I actually ended up making alot less in 2019 than I planned, by almost $100,000. This is because I changed careers from an incredibly stressful consulting role where I was traveling 100% to something that enabled me to be home everyday. Again, not planned in 2018, but a definite implication to the pay off plan. In hindsight I do not regret this at all because our income is now on the upside, which leads me to my next point: Taking a risk.

By June 2020 we still owed ~$47,000 of student loan debt. COVID was in full motion and candidly we thought it would take us until the October or maybe December 2020 to pay off the balance..a 3rd extension. But boom, in the middle of covid, my wife's business takes off. She gets a major client, and just like that we have an extra ~$35,000 influx of cash that we could potentially apply to our student loan pay off balance. Candidly she has been pursuing her side hustle/turned business for over 24 months, this was not an 'overnight windfall', but rather a culmination of many small iterations/events over a 2 year window.

We actually sat on this cash for a couple weeks, unsure if it was a good idea to pay off this debt in the middle of COVID. But candidly, logging into earnest every morning , at 8am, on the dot, and seeing that damn student loan balance was just too much. Looking back we don't regret this at all. It's incredibly lifting, freeing, almost spiritual, to wake up in the morning knowing you owe no one nothing, nada, zip , zilch, zero.

All in, we made a total of 67 payments across a 24 month window that started in July 2018 and ended in July 2020.

Date	Payment Amount	Applied to Principal	Applied to Interest	% Principal	% Interest
7/18/2018	$700.00	$697.44	$2.56	99.63%	0.37%
7/18/2018	$100.00	$1.62	$98.38	1.62%	98.38%
7/18/2018	$1,510.57	$1,134.69	$375.88	75.12%	24.88%
8/10/2018	$1,527.32	$945.60	$581.72	61.91%	38.09%
8/10/2018	$72.68	$69.85	$2.83	96.11%	3.89%
9/18/2018	$2,002.00	$1,765.92	$236.08	88.21%	11.79%
10/5/2018	$2,002.00	$1,982.09	$19.91	99.01%	0.99%
11/21/2018	$2,002.00	$1,150.80	$851.20	57.48%	42.52%
12/10/2018	$2,000.02	$725.53	$1,274.49	36.28%	63.72%
1/3/2019	$862.56	$643.45	$219.11	74.60%	25.40%
1/7/2019	$1,139.44	$1,127.49	$11.95	98.95%	1.05%
2/5/2019	$2,002.49	$1,110.84	$891.65	55.47%	44.53%
3/6/2019	$1,731.03	$953.60	$777.43	55.09%	44.91%
3/13/2019	$270.97	$222.64	$48.33	82.16%	17.84%
4/1/2019	$3,133.04	$2,294.15	$838.89	73.22%	26.78%
4/17/2019	$724.78	$682.89	$41.89	94.22%	5.78%
4/29/2019	$9,407.73	$9,381.92	$25.81	99.73%	0.27%
4/30/2019	$821.37	$820.65	$0.72	99.91%	0.09%
5/1/2019	$132.09	$131.50	$0.59	99.55%	0.45%
5/2/2019	$2,002.00	$1,218.81	$783.19	60.88%	39.12%
5/21/2019	$3,679.73	$3,607.30	$72.43	98.03%	1.97%
5/3/2019	$4,512.16	$4,474.69	$37.47	99.17%	0.83%
6/1/2019	$2,002.18	$1,303.88	$698.30	65.12%	34.88%
6/17/2019	$689.13	$653.05	$36.08	94.76%	5.24%
7/3/2019	$2,002.00	$1,367.08	$634.92	68.29%	31.71%
7/8/2019	$2,116.72	$2,100.05	$16.67	99.21%	0.79%
8/9/2019	$6,000.06	$5,197.71	$802.35	86.63%	13.37%
9/2/2019	$5,135.45	$5,099.22	$36.23	99.29%	0.71%
9/5/2019	$2,025.21	$1,367.43	$657.78	67.52%	32.48%
9/23/2019	$2,966.59	$2,903.56	$63.03	97.88%	2.12%
9/30/2019	$3,219.49	$2,750.84	$468.65	85.44%	14.56%
10/2/2019	$500.00	$494.50	$5.50	98.90%	1.10%
10/7/2019	$124.71	$111.36	$13.35	89.30%	10.70%
10/14/2019	$15,000.00	$14,981.40	$18.60	99.88%	0.12%
11/1/2019	$2,002.00	$1,425.07	$576.93	71.18%	28.82%
11/6/2019	$174.39	$172.59	$1.80	98.97%	1.03%
12/6/2019	$2,000.00	$1,851.40	$148.60	92.57%	7.43%
12/15/2019	$2,126.06	$2,044.05	$82.01	96.14%	3.86%
12/19/2019	$67.57	$31.90	$35.67	47.21%	52.79%
12/22/2019	$2,800.00	$2,773.24	$26.76	99.04%	0.96%
1/9/2020	$2,306.42	$2,150.65	$155.77	93.25%	6.75%
1/11/2020	$386.00	$369.72	$16.28	95.78%	4.22%
1/14/2020	$1,788.19	$1,763.03	$25.16	98.59%	1.41%
1/15/2020	$572.68	$564.46	$8.22	98.56%	1.44%
1/19/2020	$100.00	$67.33	$32.67	67.33%	32.67%
1/31/2020	$963.57	$963.57	$0.00	100.00%	0.00%
2/2/2020	$232.00	$223.92	$8.08	96.52%	3.48%
2/4/2020	$1,788.00	$1,771.88	$16.12	99.10%	0.90%
2/5/2020	$3,865.00	$3,857.11	$7.89	99.80%	0.20%
2/7/2020	$1,999.00	$1,983.94	$15.06	99.25%	0.75%
2/10/2020	$1,500.00	$1,500.00	$0.00	100.00%	0.00%
2/10/2020	$1,500.00	$1,477.92	$22.08	98.53%	1.47%
2/15/2020	$500.00	$464.69	$35.31	92.94%	7.06%
3/3/2020	$1,788.19	$1,668.88	$119.31	93.33%	6.67%
3/19/2020	$211.81	$102.02	$109.79	48.17%	51.83%
4/3/2020	$1,788.19	$1,685.42	$102.77	94.25%	5.75%
4/4/2020	$267.64	$260.95	$6.69	97.50%	2.50%
4/17/2020	$5,760.39	$5,673.70	$86.69	98.50%	1.50%
4/25/2020	$8,500.00	$8,450.94	$49.06	99.42%	0.58%
4/29/2020	$476.07	$454.73	$21.34	95.52%	4.48%
5/2/2020	$549.07	$549.01	$0.06	99.99%	0.01%
5/3/2020	$1,788.19	$1,767.02	$21.17	98.82%	1.18%
5/16/2020	$5,000.00	$4,934.01	$65.99	98.68%	1.32%
6/3/2020	$1,788.19	$1,705.23	$82.96	95.36%	4.64%
7/3/2020	$1,788.19	$1,654.73	$133.46	92.54%	7.46%
7/17/2020	$45,576.20	$45,516.10	$60.10	99.87%	0.13%
7/18/2020	$4.29	$4.29	$0.00	100.00%	0.00%

With principal and interest, the total payback amount was $184,030.12. If we took the 10 year standard payment plan, the payback amount would have been >$240,000. No thanks. Our average payment on a monthly basis was around $7,357. More details below:

Average	$7,357.72
Median	$2,691.31
Low	$1,600.00
High	$45,580.49
Interest Paid	$12,109.08
Principal Paid	$171,921.04
Total Payback Amount	$184,030.12
Months to payoff	24

Final conclusion: It is possible.

My educated and broke journey started in 2018 as a personal financial experiment. It was really a running joke I had with my coworkers. We collectively agreed that there was a generation of young people who were really educated but really broke. It wasn't until months later, did I realize that I was one of them. When I began to engage my friends, family and coworkers about the role of student loan debt in society, the response was mostly apathetic. Everyone thought it was "normal", and technically they were right. As of August 2020, 80% of American can't afford an emergency that costs > $500. 1

out 4 of Americans have more in debt that in retirement, 60% of americans will die with debt, and the average car loan is $508 on a 72 month note.

But you don't have to choose apathy. The harsh realization is that the government is not going to "wipe our student loan debt" free. I wish they would. I wish our elected officials would take the time to reevaulate the role of the Federal student loan program, college tuition, and access to affordable education. But sadly It took a global pandemic and economic collapse that impacted almost 300,000,000 american citizens for our elected officials to approve a $2 trillion dollar stimulus package. Compare that to the 45 million americans who collectively owe $1.3 trillion in outstanding student loan debt. It is (sadly) clear that the $1.3 trillion dollars of student loan debt is not considered a macro economic crisis that will impact the US economy. It might impact the economics of your house, of my house…but that isn't enough to get the attention of the government.

But it is possible to pay off your student loan debt. This is proof. You may roll your eyes after reading this… "easy for you to say, you have a dual income household with no kids and make a bunch of money". I definitely heard that alot. I ask you to not just to look at the numbers, but also evaluate the intent. The intent of living on a written budget where you spend less than you make and work with your husband/wife/spouse/self to set and achieve a goal.

This book is my contribution to 45 million Americans looking for an answer to their student loan problem. To the educated and broke, those high income earners with college degrees but no savings, the doctors, the lawyers, engineers, educators and everyone in between: commit to no consumer debt, make a written budget before the start of the month, and aim to live off of 60% of your post tax income. You were not born to work, pay bills, and die.

John
San Francisco, California
August 2020

REFERENCES

This is $170,000 of student loan debt.

1. Oyedele, A. (2017, February 17). Americans have $12.58 trillion of debt - here's what it looks like. Retrieved July 14, 2020, from https://www.businessinsider.com/us-household-debt-credit-ny-fed-q4-2016-2017-2

2. Board of Governors of the Federal Reserve System. (n.d.). Retrieved July 14, 2020, from https://www.federalreserve.gov/releases/g19/current/

3. Americans Have So Much Debt They're Taking It to The Grave. (n.d.). Retrieved July 14, 2020, from https://money.com/americans-die-in-debt/

4. Writer, A. (2019, November 07). The U.S. Consumer Debt Crisis. Retrieved July 14, 2020, from https://www.debt.org/faqs/americans-in-debt/

5. SoFi. (2019, September 24). The Growing Student Loan Default Rate. Retrieved July 14,

2020, from https://www.sofi.com/learn/content/student-loan-default-rate/

6. AnnieReporter. (2018, December 21). Here are the facts about public service loan forgiveness. Retrieved July 14, 2020, from https://www.cnbc.com/2018/12/21/1-percent-of-people-were-approved-for-public-service-loan-forgiveness.html

7. Friedman, Z. (2019, October 14). Student Loan Debt Statistics In 2018: A $1.5 Trillion Crisis. Retrieved July 14, 2020, from https://www.forbes.com/sites/zackfriedman/2018/06/13/student-loan-debt-statistics-2018/

Why your car loan cost you $5.2 million dollars

1. Kyle Morgan link. (2019, November 02). Car loan statistics 2020: Americans owe $1.3 trillion in auto debt. Retrieved July 14, 2020, from https://www.finder.com/car-loan-statistics

FICO: The Greatest American Scam of all time

1. Resendiz, J. (2020, June 17). Average Credit Card Debt in America: July 2020. Retrieved July 14, 2020, from https://www.valuepenguin.com/average-credit-card-debt

2. Peterson, B. (2019, July 15). Credit Card Spending Studies (2018 Report): Why You Spend More When You Pay With a Credit Card. Retrieved July 14, 2020, from https://www.valuepenguin.com/credit-cards/credit-card-spending-studies

3. Backman, M. (2018, February 15). It's Official: Most Americans Are Currently in Debt. Retrieved July 14, 2020, from https://www.fool.com/retirement/2018/02/15/its-official-most-americans-are-currently-in-debt.aspx

4. LaMagna, M. (2018, February 25). 1 in 5 Americans have more credit-card debt than savings. Retrieved July 14, 2020, from https://www.marketwatch.com/story/1-in-5-americans-have-more-credit-card-debt-than-savings-2018-02-22

5. 2018 Credit Card Debt Statistics: Average U.S. Debt. (2020, June 18). Retrieved July 14, 2020, from https://www.cardrates.com/advice/credit-card-debt-statistics/

The student loan interest tax deduction is a scam.

1. Song, J. (2019, September 17). Average Student Loan Debt in America: 2019 Facts & Figures. Retrieved July 16, 2020, from https://www.valuepenguin.com/average-student-loan-debt

2. Publication 970 (2019), Tax Benefits for Education. (n.d.). Retrieved July 16, 2020, from https://www.irs.gov/publications/p970

3. Picchi, A. (2017, January 12). A $500 surprise expense would put most Americans into debt. Retrieved July 16, 2020, from https://www.cbsnews.com/news/most-americans-cant-afford-a-500-emergency-expense/

4. Writer, A. (2019, December 05). Consumer Debt Statistics & Demographics in America. Retrieved July 16, 2020, from https://www.debt.org/faqs/americans-in-debt/demographics/

5. Average Car Loan Debt Statistics 2020. (n.d.). Retrieved July 16, 2020, from https://www.lendingtree.com/auto/debt-statistics/

Pay off student loans before you contribute to your 401k.

1. Shin, L. (2015, October 12). The Retirement Crisis: Why 68% Of Americans Aren't Saving In An Employer-Sponsored Plan. Retrieved July 18, 2020, from https://www.forbes.com/sites/laurashin/2015/04/09/the-retirement-crisis-why-68-of-americans-arent-saving-in-an-employer-sponsored-plan/

2. Friedman, Z. (2019, October 14). Student Loan Debt Statistics In 2018: A $1.5 Trillion Crisis. Retrieved July 18, 2020, from https://www.forbes.com/sites/zackfriedman/2018/06/13/student-loan-debt-statistics-2018/

3. Kyle Morgan link. (2019, November 02). Car loan statistics 2020: Americans owe $1.3 trillion in auto debt. Retrieved July 18, 2020, from https://www.finder.com/car-loan-statistics

4. 401(k) contribution limit increases to $19,000 for 2019; IRA limit increases to $6,000. (n.d.). Retrieved July 18, 2020, from https://www.irs.gov/newsroom/401k-contribution-limit-increases-to-19000-for-2019-ira-limit-increases-to-6000

5. (n.d.). Retrieved July 18, 2020, from https://www.federalreserve.gov/econres/scfindex.htm

6. (n.d.). Retrieved July 18, 2020, from https://www.earnest.com/invite/john8602

The government will not forgive your debt.

1. (n.d.). Retrieved July 18, 2020, from https://www.cbo.gov/system/files?file=2019-05/51310-2019-05-studentloan.pdf

Control your money with a budget

1. Peterson, B. (2019, July 15). Credit Card Spending Studies (2018 Report): Why You Spend More When You Pay With a Credit Card. Retrieved September 07, 2020, from https://www.valuepenguin.com/credit-cards/credit-card-spending-studies

ABOUT THE AUTHOR

Born in the Republic of the Philippines in 1986, John migrated to Sacramento, California with his mother in the pursuit of the American dream. Growing up in abject poverty, John had a front row seat to the damage caused due to a lack of financial education. It wasn't 2018, after graduating from the Unviersity of Southern California with an MBA, did John learn the framework required for true wealth creation.

To his good fortune, John had the opportunity to seek the wisdom and mentorship of elders, self-made millionaires, and captains of industry who all echoed similar stories on their path to wealth creation. This book chronicles how John leveraged his lessons-learned to overcome the shackles of student loan debt and a decade of poor money management on his journey to debt-freedom and wealth creation.

John lives in San Francisco, California with his wife Rosalind.

www.ingramcontent.com/pod-product-compliance
Lightning Source LLC
Chambersburg PA
CBHW020440220526
45464CB00002B/781